# FINNS

# FINNS

## 27 YEARS ON CHELSEA GREEN

*Julia Bannister*

THE LOGAN PRESS

2012

This book has been designed and typeset
in Monotype Joanna by Patrick Roe.
The printing and binding have been carried out by
The Fine Book Bindery of Wellingborough
on Stow Ivory Book Wove paper.

This limited edition consists of 999 numbered copies
of which 918 are bound in quarter cloth
and 81 quarter bound in leather.

ISBN 9780946988099

Finns of Chelsea Green

Established 1985
One Family, Two Generations

Finns of Chelsea Green
a Kitchen, a Shop, a Café, a Life

THIS IS COPY NUMBER

Julia, age 5.

Photography: Norman Chalk.

Milly, age 5.

Photograph: Richard Greenly Photography.

# For Mothers and Daughters

For my Mother
without whom there would be no marmalade

For Louise
without whom there would be no Milly

# Contents

# Foreword

by Nicholas Shakespeare

Julia's habit of enchanting everyone on whom she turns her samphire-green eyes is common knowledge. I was doubly susceptible after discovering that we have a curious and unusual link. We both have a mother called Lalage (from the Greek word for "prattler"). Not only that, but Julia's father was present at the very instant when my mother met my father in Oxford on Wednesday 25 April 1951.

The other day my mother produced a remarkable photograph which captures this coup de foudre. It shows my parents-to-be standing in Christ Church's Tom Quad, part of a group called Undergrad Tours which was formed to take Americans around Oxford colleges during the Festival of Britain. One of the original founders and guides was Julia's father, Andrew Talbot Rice, who, as though aware of what is unravelling a few feet away, glances over at my mother, who is employed as the secretary. She stands beside a young undergraduate from Trinity College introduced to her only moments before — my father — who has been hired as another guide. Forty years on, in one of many gratifying symmetries, Julia was to steer tours of Americans around Rome.

Julia and I also met in Oxford. I remember parties at Christ Church, the Hellfire Caves at West Wykeham, Adwell and weekends at Coombe House where I came to know Julia's strikingly beautiful mother, Lalage.

One Christmas, we both had jobs at Harrods. As Julia worked upstairs in Table to Ovenware, I, out of sight, plucked turkeys and pheasants down in the Harrods' basement. At lunchtime, I would climb the back staircase to the fifth floor and meet Julia in the staff canteen. She was selling dinner services and lasagne dishes, staple presents for the weddings of our Oxford friends in London, Northumberland and Scotland which Julia and I found ourselves attending together.

Left to right: Michael Barsley, Barry Johnson, Martin Stevens, Christopher Johnson
(standing), Andrew Talbot Rice, Suzette Villar, Lalage Mayes, John Shakespeare.

We hatched a plan one hot summer with my great school friend, Piers Litherland, who had since become Julia's great friend, to go to Italy as a trio. Piers and I plotted to show Julia those parts of Italy she had not visited yet. We would show her Carpaccio's panels of St Jerome in Venice, Duccio's Maestà in Siena, Piero della Francesca's frescoes in Arezzo. We had no money. We would do it – as usual – "più economica." But we would do it royally and gather our mushrooms, so to speak, until our baskets were full. Sadly, Julia slipped through our fingers and our Italian trip never materialised. Piers went into banking via the Far East, I went into journalism and broadcasting via the BBC, and Julia went into wet fish via Bond Street.

Our paths did not cross again until, on a fishing trip in Lancashire's Trough of Bowland, I was told by the owner of the inn where I was staying that Julia lived locally. I rang her up and drove over to Coniston where, in a cottage by the river Aire, I found her married with three boys and surrounded by casserole dishes. She told me that she was now running a food shop in Chelsea.

It wasn't until I was visiting the novelist William Boyd for lunch nearby that I finally stumbled across Julia's emporium on Chelsea Green. It turned out that Will bought his picnics for the rugby at Twickenham from Finns. In another pleasing twist, Finns was located right next to what was once a grocer's owned by my uncle, a mushroom farmer in Wittering, who used it as an outlet for his produce. I swiftly discovered that lots of people I knew used Finns for covert catering. As soon as I saw Julia through the window, standing behind the till, I walked in – just as streams of people who were once in prams have come through that door, some now pushing prams. She says, looking back over an enterprise that has flourished now for almost three decades and shows no evidence of wilting: "I am endlessly surprised at the changing scenes of life, the criss-cross of people and generations, of time and place. It keeps happening in Finns."

For the past four years, my family and I have shared holidays with Julia in Pieve di Brancoli in the hills above Lucca. On our bikes, beside the pool, over an aperitif, my wife, Gillian, sketches and builds a portfolio of drawings to pepper the pages of this book. We talk about the trends in food, the different dishes that people buy, the busy lives of the people who come into the shop, the occasions at which they cater, the travels that Julia makes in search of ceramics, hand-painted china and the gifts they sell at Finns for presents. We talk about coincidences, the Lalages, our lives, and the life of Finns. We discuss what to call Julia's book, its timeline, its big wheel of repetition.

# Acknowledgements

Thank you to all our customers. At whatever point in the past twenty-seven years you discovered Finns, I thank you for your enthusiasm, encouragement, friendship, criticisms and, most importantly, for your loyalty.

The idea of this book would never have gone from head to paper without two very important partnerships.

From an artistic and literary household in Edinburgh, Griselda Murray Brown came to Finns armed with an English degree from Oxford and a burning determination to work in journalism. For three months we researched together, read together and wrote together. We met literary agents, publishers and printers. Her gentle and calm disposition belies a steely wit and quiet determination. The day she left to work for the *Weekend Financial Times*, was their gain and our loss. The Finns book project went on hold.

It lay dormant in my trusty Trussardi rucksack until an old friend of mine proffered her daughter, Eliza Grant, to be a cook at Finns. There was, literally, no space available in the kitchen or the shop but, drawn by the enthusiasm and charm of this clever, funny and anxious graduate, it seemed the time was right to dust off the unfinished copy and pick up where Griselda had left off. From a large musical and literary household in Glasgow, she came armed with an English degree from Cambridge and a burning determination to work for the Metropolitan Police. Eliza's primary mission was to drive the book forward and she has unstintingly embraced this challenge. I am eternally grateful for the patience with which she has pored and picked over draft after draft, accompanied me to printers, publishers and book fairs, interviewed artists, photographers and graphic designers and presented her findings each day.

Both Griselda and Eliza completely understood the brief and shared the same vision for the look, feel and content of the book. Without them I would never have had the confidence to pursue it.

To Milly, for her gentle ways and limitless energy, her selflessness and quiet ambition, her patience and her sense of fun. She has shared in the future of Finns wholeheartedly. The shop is a better place for her presence.

To all the girls at Finns: Katie Mitchell, Colette Robert, Marina Power, Rosa Banbury and Marisa Ramos. They are the making of it each day.

To all the girls who have worked there over the past twenty-seven years. In particular Beth Stuart-Findlay who generously lent me her photographs taken during the early years of Finns; Tanya Ware, Christine Du Toit and Fiona Bodles. I thank all four for their dedication and passion.

To all the young who have done work experience at Finns: Frances Buchanan, Tom Bannister, Juliet Tollemache, Clemmie Gaisman, Stephanie Evans, Emma Varley, Florence Fox-Andrews, Alice Kelway-Bamber, Charlotte Brook, Helen Crosbie-Dawson, Paddy Pilkington, Daisy Francklin, Alice Bowring, Marina Stephens, Imogen Stagg.

To Nicholas and Gillian Shakespeare. Nicholas for his unstinting encouragement and joyous foreword. To Gillian for her beautiful pen and ink drawings, her readiness to illustrate the story and the skill with which she has done so.

I would like to thank my children, Harry, Archie and Roddy. Many people dedicate their books to their children for their enthusiasm, interest and help. Mine have shown remarkably little interest and helped not one bit but they bring Nick and me the greatest pleasure and joy in every other way.

To my brothers and sister, Richard, Jono and Catherine. Through all the changing scenes of life, they have been my constants.

To my mother and my father upon whom I lean so heavily and whose love and guidance for me and my children has been extraordinary.

# Introduction

In 1985 a quail's egg was rare. A picnic was a hard boiled egg with salad cream, a floury bap and a wizened drumstick. An upmarket picnic was a smoked salmon sandwich, veal and ham pie, Dundee cake and an apple. Twenty-seven years on, a picnic can be a catered event as competitive for the provider as for the child in the egg and spoon race.

In 1985, the concept of paying for ready-made food was an alien one. People cooked or employed a cook. 'Celebrities' did not exist: they were famous people. Recipe books were practical and proven. They were used long after the pages had left the spine and people treasured and traded recipes. Most food was seasonal, little was imported and a bag of pre-washed salad available from a garage forecourt was unimaginable. There was very little waste.

Food shoppers, women in the main, shopped for fuel not fun and bought what they could carry. Food shops closed at 5pm and never opened on a Sunday. Apart from Harrods Food Hall, Fortnum & Mason, Partridges and Justin de Blank, there were few high-end purveyors of food in London. Supermarkets were not synonymous with ready-cooked meals, they were more about value than quality or diversity of products; they sold affordable staples and were not the all inclusive, twenty-four hour shopping experience we have come to rely on. Coffee shops and sandwich bars were mainly independent, nothing like the glut of brands which punctuate our streets today. Farmers' markets sold livestock in rural auction marts, not the exciting variety of artisan produce that now ventures to London each week. Delicatessens, mainly Continental, sold cold meats, tins and exotics. Olive oil was available in small bottles from chemists. Vegetarianism was cranky, allergies and food intolerances not tolerated.

Most cooks were unaware of the delights of Lebanese, Turkish and Moroccan cuisines. Pomegranates, preserved lemons, hummus, harissa and spices were more Manna than manifest. Lentils, chickpeas, pulses and grains were rarely used; avocados were a treat. The tearing, tossing and roasting of Tuscan vegetables was as new wave as balsamic vinegar and pesto; Thai flavours and fusion food still continents away.

A tray of cocktail eats comprised of pinwheels of tinned asparagus wrapped in brown bread, small triangles of parfait and aspic, and platters of mushroom vol-au-vents. Starters on a restaurant menu included Florida cocktail, prawn cocktail, whitebait and a selection of juices – tomato, orange, pineapple. Salads saw raw green pepper religiously diced into rice, sweetcorn added for further colour and interest. Vegetables were thoroughly cooked – Al Dente an unknown Italian gentleman; steak Diane a favourite and Black Forest Gâteau to impress.

It was against this background that Kevin and Livvie Cooper and I opened Finns, a 343 square foot English gourmet food store. Our plan was to sell a selection of dishes cooked on the premises throughout the day. Every dish would be made in small amounts with no shortcuts, using ingredients collected from the markets each morning. Into an already small kitchen, we

installed a large walk-in chill room. Here we stored ingredients as they were delivered, dishes and orders as they were completed and it served as a place of refuge when the heat was truly on.

Finns is situated on Elystan Street, the shortest side of a triangle that is known as Chelsea Green. Small dogs stretch their legs on the green grass, bicycles lean against the iron railings, slatted wooden benches support passers-by, and a cherry blossom stands showering residents, poets, pensioners and picnickers with its fragrant pink flowers. Before the Enclosures Act of the 18th century, Chelsea Green provided grazing for the livestock of Box Farm, long since buried under Markham and Elystan Streets. One splendid Chelsea denizen, Lady Rusteen Wynne-Jones, campaigned for many years for the residents to continue to exercise their grazing rights and have a goat on the Green. She fought too for the installation of a fountain with roses and geraniums and a pond filled with trout where children could fish.

Chelsea Green has the feel of a village. Almost complete with butcher, baker and candlestick maker, it is a diverse and vibrant community. Many of the shop faces change but the feel of working and living on Chelsea Green remains the same. The shopkeepers, professionals and residents who live and work around the Green make up the cocktail of nationalities, ages and incomes which can be found here on a daily basis. Elegant residents leave the portered flats of Cranmer Court and join the shoppers from the doorways of the labyrinth red brick Sutton Trust Dwellings; children and nannies spill from the colourful houses and cottages which lead to Chelsea Green.

It is in Finns that those in the know take refuge from the busy maelstrom of the King's Road. The shop has often been compared to 84 Charing Cross Road for its individuality and intimacy, for its own personality and the personalities it supplies.

The opening of this small store was a huge venture. Whilst we were ahead of the culinary game, the game was enormously difficult. Twenty-seven years on, urged and cajoled by our customers, this book will reveal the enduring recipes of the shop. More than that, it may serve as a springboard for armchair shopkeepers who dream of starting their own food shop but do not believe they can.

As I sit in Finns enclosed by the asparagus green walls, writing this book and surrounded by familiar faces, I marvel at how it has all worked out.

Three decades, two generations, one family.

# The Book

This book has been a long time in the making. The various avenues down which I have wandered have been interesting and distracting in equal measure. There were so many decisions to make.

The first was whether to seek to be published or to self-publish. It was the legendary Piers Russell-Cobb who, when the book was embryonic, introduced me to the world of publishing in all its guises. An audience with a leading publisher revealed I would have to trade the quirks and idiosyncrasies of Finns to broaden the book's appeal and reach readers from Stockholm to Sydney. It was suggested that I write for a more international audience and not with the existing customers in mind. This was not a compromise I felt comfortable making and at this point self-publishing became increasingly attractive. In this way, the book would be a product of the people who worked at Finns, the recipes tried, tested and proven over the years. No-one who had not been intimately connected with the shop would determine how the book would read and look. We would be our own editors, proof readers and home economists, our own kitchen the test kitchen, our customers our panel. Whilst I knew it would take longer, I felt this collaborative effort would be more personal and more authentic.

As the project got underway, I started to read cookery books from cover to cover. I made frequent visits to Book Thrift in South Kensington and Books for Cooks in Notting Hill Gate. I began to get a feel for the shelf life of a recipe book and a pattern soon emerged: the books that stayed in my head longest were less glossy and more understated.

Now the cookery book has become a coffee table feast for the eye, woe betide the splash back from real cooking. Too often, cooking is more about flowery prints than floury fingers. Many modern cookery books have become testimonies to a perceived lifestyle. They have large glamourous photographs

of chickens and Gloucester Old Spots with names from *Upstairs Downstairs*, glorious views, good-looking dogs and carefully chosen children parting fields of barley wearing new clothes bought to look like hand-me-downs. Stone-washed, indeed. Which river? That is why I find the traditional cookery books from my mother's shelves the more enjoyable reads. I admire authors like Elizabeth David, Katie Stewart, Arabella Boxer, Josceline Dimbleby and Elisabeth Luard – the practicality of their kitchens, their personal journeys, their graft and their grit and, above all, the conviction which shines through their recipes.

Whilst full of admiration for the tricks and styling of modern day food photography, I am more charmed by the grainy matt photographs of grey stews illuminated only by piped mashed potato and cleverly turned carrots. In the end, for this book, I decided to eschew photographs of food and focus on the photographs which illustrate the life of Finns.

I began meeting with printers. I needed to find someone who understood the project and could create the book I had in mind: something that was a pleasure to hold yet practical, something that emphasised the passage of time and yet would stand the test of time.

There was no end to the way in which the book could be presented, with spiral binding, a book in a box, separate recipe cards and many more ideas presenting themselves as options. I interviewed book designers over cups of coffee at Finns and travelled further afield to book fairs and studios all over

England. I got quotes from China, paper samples from India, endpapers from Italy. We talked and talked to customers and were steered by many of you who felt very strongly that the book should be produced and printed in England. Thus, after many months of searching for someone who was a perfect fit for this all-consuming project, I started making regular visits to Patrick Roe and the team at the Fine Book Bindery in Wellingborough. The company comprises of those who have dedicated their working lives to making beautiful, handmade bespoke books. In his busy factory, I walked amongst reams of paper, bolts of cloth and other materials used to make book covers and Solander boxes; I sifted through bundles of leather for the more luxurious bindings and marvelled at the multitudinous metal plates and type-faces tucked away in long wooden drawers. I was shown the Victorian printing presses which Patrick restores at the weekends and met the team who take such pride in the books they produce: Frances, Bet, Bob, Brian, Kevin, Malcolm, Mandy, Marilyn and Mark. In Patrick, I finally found someone who would be able to express the longevity and charm of Finns. Over the summer months, he and his small team have carefully designed, crafted and hand bound each individual Finns book. I am truly grateful to them all for absorbing the specification so deliberately.

# The Early Years

At fifty-three I find, to my eternal surprise, that I have devoted my working life to a delicatessen on Chelsea Green. As a young adult, I had envisaged a career in the art world, aspiring to curate a museum or work as a researcher in the Witt library for which my qualifications, such as they were, had prepared me. I had no desire to cook or ever dreamed of running a shop. But, for twenty-seven years, I have lived and worked in The Royal Borough of Kensington and Chelsea amongst the great and the good, the safe and the wild, the traders and the residents who make up this small community. Finns has seen me through the vagaries of marriage, three children and divorce. It is hard to think of any other business that would have accommodated the highs and lows of these busy years so patiently and with such humour. There have been times when it has been tempting to sell, especially when faced with attractive offers from aspiring shopkeepers, but as my parents point out, Finns defines me. Despite the protestations of my more erudite friends – how dreadful to be defined by a delicatessen – I am very glad it does.

Born in Cheyne Row, I started life in Chelsea in a neighbourhood which has housed a great number of distinguished residents: from Thomas Carlyle and Dante Gabriel Rossetti, who was banned from keeping his peacocks due to the din, to Mick Jagger, another glorious peacock with much to shout about. Little did I know that one more Chelsea neighbour, Elizabeth David, would, twenty years later, become one of Finns' first and most critical customers. The day she ordered ham for Christmas was a landmark in our early years.

Although born in Chelsea, my three siblings and I were brought up in Barnes. My father was a stockbroker and my mother was a mother. We were lavished with love but plenty and excess were not synonymous with my childhood. It was not an austere household but we practised what Elizabeth

Gaskell, an erstwhile resident of Chelsea, termed "elegant economy" and "one or none" was the general cry.

I have happy memories of time spent with my mother in the kitchen. A very good cook, she took pleasure in preparing our childhood meals and creating a repertoire of family favourites. Always a tablecloth on the table at breakfast and napkins in silver rings, we ate meals together punctuated by elevenses, high tea and honey-milk before bed. I particularly remember the wonderful pies and puddings my mother made us, dishes now rather tiresomely referred to as "nostalgia food." Steak and kidney, corned beef hash, fish pie with lots of egg, lamb hotpot with dumplings, hearty casseroles and stuffed marrow rings with mince and grated cheese – my favourite.

Our larder was full of home made chutneys and jellies and a large platter housed the left over joint from Sunday lunch which would be reinvented in many guises before the bones and carcasses were made into stocks for soup. I loved helping make meringues and crumbles, trifles and fruit fools. We made the presents we gave at Christmas: peppermint creams tinted with pale pink and ice-green food colouring, clove studded orange pomanders with pretty ribbons and cellophane bundles of fudge tied with raffia.

We had a wonderful Nanny, Jean Foubister, who came from the Black Isle to live with us for twenty-five years. Together we made shortbread rounds onto which we pressed a thistle stamp. We rolled butter balls with her wooden butter paddles and made drop scones on the Aga to eat with bramble jelly. I learnt to make profiteroles of shiny choux pastry which we stuffed with whipped cream, tinned mandarins and topped with glistening dark chocolate. My other childhood food memories are of times shared with my dearly beloved grandmother, Lal Buchanan. Creative and imaginative, she had raised my mother in Kenya and Rhodesia. Her cooking was resourceful and inventive. Soups and broths, their eclectic contents enhanced by the intense stocks in which they bobbed, were always referred to as SOS: Soup of Sorts. We made oatcakes from goose fat and marmalade she called GLOM: Grapefruit, Lemon, Orange, Marmalade. For each batch, she cut a goldfish out of orange peel and placed one in every jam jar. It was always a thrill to be the one who spotted the goldfish on the spoon.

We spent our holidays in the Somerset Quantocks on day long bike rides with picnics in our saddle bags and baskets: ham sandwiches, hard boiled eggs, squashed fly biscuits and a sherbet fountain. We picked and ate whortleberries, made bracken houses with sheath knives, built dams in the sparkling streams and jumped the mossy bogs. We made corn dollies and lavender spindles with satin ribbon and no-one knew or asked where we were. Latterly we drove to Brittany where I loved the festivals and processions of the *Filets Bleus* with stout Breton ladies in tall lace hats and children in embroidered skirts dancing and singing beside their elaborate floats. It was

there that I first tried shellfish and my memories are of crabs, mussels and piles of langoustines with mustard mayonnaise followed by crêpes and brûlées, fresh greengages, orange melons and bright red cherries.

I left my school, Downe House, at sixteen with better friends than qualifications. Whilst not expelled, I was encouraged to leave by a rather fatigued headmistress. This coincided with a family move to Oxford where I attended Beech Lawn for a glorious and unheard of six hours of lessons a week. I travelled by underpowered red moped, punctuating my time with punting, cooking, poetry and piano. It was an intensely happy period during which I pushed every boundary that came my way and I believed that everything was possible.

I left at eighteen and flew to Florence to spend three months in Italy where my diet veered from the sublime to the ridiculous. I P.G'd with an impoverished Contessa and we dined on quantities of polenta which the Italian cook relentlessly prepared for us. We longed for risotto, pasta and

grilled meats but such delights rarely appeared. We strolled the narrow streets, sauntered in and out of galleries and churches and spent evenings in cafés carefully parting with five hundred lire notes in exchange for four-inch squares of pizza. Later there was ice-cream from Vivolis and cups of thick hot chocolate with whipped cream in the Piazza Santo Spirito, tastes and memories I will never forget.

A long and happy weekend was spent picking grapes at a sprawling vineyard near Orbetello. With a large hooked blade on our forefingers and panniers on our backs, we worked the rows of grapes in the hot sunshine while tractors drove up and down the vines collecting our laden panniers. Students from every country had been lured by the offer of free food and wine and we sat up through the night singing Italian songs and drinking endless carafes of rough red wine with hunks of bread and chunks of salami.

Impatient to travel, together with a fellow P.G., Vicky Saunders, we threw in the towel at the Dante Alighieri Institute and hitch-hiked from Florence to Venice with no money, no fear and no plan. It was on a cold, misty and damp November day that we found ourselves taking refuge in a freezing cold and spartan convent on Giudecca. Determined to drink Bellinis and eat small sandwiches at Harry's Bar, but safe in the knowledge that this cost an arm and a leg, we had to think on our feet. We had seen many a beggar on the Ponte Vecchio shake out his missing limb and stroll off in pursuit of Grappa. Impressed by this route to riches, we wrote a long sign on the convent's hard loo paper *siamo deaf mute sensa madre e padre* (we are deaf mute without mother or father) and set about begging on the steps of San Marco. Five hours later,

much to our amazement, our stair was bare. Whether it was Vicky's paper anorak emblazoned with *Ski Les Trois Vallées* or the endless cheerful chatter from these deaf mutes that deterred any generous benefactors, we will never know.

The fruits of our hair-raising and in hindsight staggeringly foolish hitch-hiking exploits landed us in Rome where we stayed as guests of the flamboyant Canadian, Danny O'Keefe Browning, a friend of Vicky's parents. In his exquisite apartment within the beautiful 16th century Palazzo Cenci in Rome's Jewish ghetto, I had frescos on my bedroom wall to rival any Giotto or Masaccio left behind in Florence. It was here that I first tried parma ham. We breakfasted on fine, slightly velvety slices accompanied by fresh figs and chestnut honey. I had never experienced anything quite like it and the delectable quality married to the exoticness of it all makes it one of my most potent food memories. Danny gave us an account with a small pizzeria across the piazza where huge wooden paddles carried wafer thin pizzas in and out of an ancient brick oven. Basil, tomatoes, capers, anchovies, roasted peppers and grilled artichokes were fresh ingredients and intense flavours so totally different to the food on which I had grown-up.

I returned to England eager to begin a job. My first was easily found, the notions of CVs, work experience and competitive interviews an anomaly in the early eighties. I began as an art gallery assistant on Bond Street, bidding at auctions, cataloguing and attempting to sell paintings. I lunched regularly with Louise Bannister who, many years later, became my sister-in-law and mother to Milly, Bella, Fred and Alice.

After two years on Bond Street, I left disillusioned by my all too often solitary day. It was time to take stock. To my horror, my father suggested that it would be character forming to volunteer my services as a waitress in a Christian café called The Well. Located opposite Victoria Coach Station, it was affiliated to St Michael's Church, Chester Square where my Uncle was the Vicar. It made available cheap and cheerful food for those who were down and out or on their uppers. The food was good but the focus was on God. For me there was no pay and I constantly harboured unChristian thoughts as the staff prayed together each night – they for others and their good fortune, me for myself and any sort of fortune. If I wanted to take any money back to my tiny flat situated above Belgravia Books, I was going to have to rely solely on tips. As such, I became swift and eager to turn tables amongst a clientèle who, in the main, had nowhere to go and scarcely a bus to catch. Taking God in my stride and with my character formed, I left, hungry to earn.

I took a temporary job as a PA to Kevin Cooper, an Irish fish merchant who, with his wife Livvie, ran a fish processing and smoking factory in Kenmare, Co. Kerry. It was an introduction to food from source, from trawler to table. One day we would be gutting salmon and grading prawns, the next we were designing labels for the smoked salmon paté we sold in Harrods.

Kenmare had a population of 1200, fed and watered by the twenty-four pubs that lined Henry Street and Main Street. I remember many lunches at The Purple Heather run by Grainne O'Connell who made a thick, rich fish

soup with whole pieces of prawn surfacing from the deep orange bisque and served in a heavy stoneware bowl with soda bread and cold Kerry butter.

Work was obsessive and intoxicating. The drive which infused Livvie and myself came from Kevin. He was impossible, inspiring, energetic, generous, unpredictable and fiercely Irish. A law unto himself, anti-British, anti-establishment, fearless in word and deed, he was the original entrepreneur. For Kevin, everything was possible.

It was into this hectic environment that Jackie Murray Brown arrived and imbued the London basement office in Jubilee House, Cadogan Place with calm, charm and much shared laughter. Imagine my delight when her daughter, Griselda, came to me twenty years later and began to record the early years of the Finns of which her mother had been such a great part. Similarly calming, charming and funny, this family continuity is what I so love about Finns.

Jackie and I ran a small mail order business selling sides of Irish smoked salmon which would arrive from the Kenmare factory in Ireland. Keen for a diversion from this very seasonal business, we devised an Irish picnic hamper, commissioning a white willow basket which we filled with the finest Waterford crystal champagne glasses, a beautiful rug from Donegal, Irish linen napkins, cutlery and silver pots for salt and pepper. The last unsold willow baskets were, for twenty-five years, our storage at Finns.

Kevin was determined that we should sell these hampers to Neimann Marcus in Texas and on this whim, Jackie and I were dispatched on our first international business trip to Dallas, armed with two hampers, six sides of smoked salmon and a flyer painted by her husband, Charlie Murray Brown. Later we pounded the pavements of New York pitching to Macy's, Zabars and

Bloomingdale's. We were enthralled by the food shops of Manhattan: The Silver Palate on Columbus Avenue, Dean and Deluca on Broadway and the many grocery marts that served fresh food. Little did we know the seeds were being sown for Finns.

Kevin and I formed a small company called Jubilee House Foods and took stands at food shows from Bloomsbury to Boston and latterly at the International Food Exhibition at Olympia. Definitely more wholesalers than retailers, we explored the market for a range of fish soups, fish patés and smoked fish products. We commissioned ceramic pots from the potteries in Stoke the size of small Patum Peperium pots into which we poured smoked fish butters. In the early years of Finns, customers bought these small pots and returned each week for them to be refilled.

In 1984 we were supplying Irish smoked salmon to the Auchan supermarket chain in France and Marks and Spencer in Ireland. We conducted our business with M&S through a remarkable and forward-thinking man named Peter Raab who gave us an insight into the changing nature of the eating and shopping habits of their clientèle. Their introduction of frozen chicken kiev had been a phenomenal success, providing a gateway to a rapidly burgeoning market for pre-prepared food and ready-meals. Armed with this knowledge and the unstinting support and encouragement of M&S, we determined to open a high-end delicatessen in the centre of London where we would provide shoppers with dishes which, and this was crucial, were cooked on the premises from which they were sold. We would supplement our range with smoked fish products from the factory in Ireland.

We knew before we began our search that Chelsea Green would be the ideal place. The combination of thirty-two independent traders making it a one stop destination for the busy housewife; a place where accounts were held, deliveries made, and traders recognised and called their customers by name. We took over an Italian delicatessen called Raphael's on Elystan Street, sandwiched between the pub and the Astell Pharmacy. The only reminders of this traditional family deli are the large butcher's hooks upon which hung their parma hams and salamis and which still punctuate the ceiling at Finns today.

We joined the likes of Bill Squires of The Chelsea Fishery. With his glad eye and keen ear for a racing tip, he would lure us beneath the pavement where the *Sporting Life* was avidly read before being wrapped around ice-fresh Dover Soles and Skate Wings and topped with a box of gulls' eggs. Fry's the Greengrocer run by Paul and Mo who displayed their fruit and vegetables with pride and sent fruit baskets to new mothers in hospital. Their son Colin washed and buffed your car whilst Reuben at Real washed and coiffed your hair.

Jago, one of the longest serving traders, a traditional family butcher selling properly hung, best cuts of English meat and game. The window displaying marbled beef, new English lamb and deeply scored pork interspersed with the first fresh game birds in season and divided by plastic grass borders. Many a gentleman has handed over a brace of pheasants in full feather to be plucked by the men in the long blue and white aprons, Big John, Little John or David himself. Suppliers to Finns for twenty-six years, they deliver to us three times each day, keep our knives sharpened and the girls in the kitchen on their toes.

Monkey's run by Tom and Brigitte Benham served potted shrimp, game birds, fine wine and brandies to a devoted clientèle including the owners of the estates on which the game birds were shot. They were Chef-Patrons in the true sense of the word. A collage of bounced cheques decorated the restaurant window, with *Refer To Drawer* stamped large serving as an effective method of naming and shaming the blaggards who had issued them. Au Bon Accueil, everybody's local, where tables were eagerly sought and quickly turned: foie de veau grillé (£7.90) a highlight amongst classic French regional dishes.

The busy corner Post Office saw two formidable ladies offer a traditional Post Office service now long forgotten. This was the era of AirMail Blueys and Poste Restante, Red Star and telex machines – e-mail, internet and mobile 'phones still pie in the sky. World's End Travel, a traditional travel agent in an era during which airline tickets were written by hand, Traveller's Cheques ordered, people smoked on aeroplanes and the Euro was an unknown four letter word.

Pietor at Lewis and Wayne: launderers, starchers and dry-cleaners of the wardrobes and bed-linen of the good and the great. Rose at the laundrette would regale us with tales of antics in the flats behind as we filled the huge machines with Finns aprons and tea-towels before inserting a waterfall of coins and a plastic cup of washing powder. A small measure of our success was when we took the corporate decision to pay the extra £6.80 a week to have a service wash.

Simmond's the hardware shop, an Aladdin's Cave of mop-heads, tools, pest control poisons and chain and rope by the yard. Wormley and Wheeler, tobacconist and newsagent, alongside newspapers and cigarettes, sold penny chews and stationery – everything from pink sugar mice to a small drawstring bag of Jacks. Matt at The Chelsea Cobbler skilled in the resoling of boots and Louboutins, engraving trophies and cutting keys. Sign of the Times, still here today, run by Lorraine with her vast knowledge of vintage, couture and nearly new designer clothes.

W.G.T. Burne sold English and Irish glass, Georgian rummers and period chandeliers. Opposite Finns are the yellow, black and white awnings of Alec Drew Picture Framers. They offered then, as they do now, a myriad choice of elaborate mounts and frames combined with careful consultation and the fine craftsmanship of David and his team.

John D Wood Estate Agents run by Andy Buchanan, the driving force behind the buying and selling of the finest houses and flats in Chelsea, as well as the organiser of the traditional Carol Service which attracts local families and friends to sing around the tree on the Green each Christmas. With mince pies and mulled wine volunteered, merriment and good voice resound.

Paul and his loyal staff at the Astell Pharmacy, dispensers of wisdom and advice for every ailment, were and have been for twenty-seven years the very best neighbours to Finns.

This was the face of Chelsea Green when we arrived. With many still trading, new faces and friends have arrived over the past twenty-seven years: Jane Asher, Robert Stephenson, Jim at Haynes Hanson and Clark, Eliza at Felt, Fifi Wilson, all our friends at Real, Claremont, David at the Paint and Paper Library, and Amaia. They all enrich the Green with their goods and services.

Chelsea Green is fast becoming a destination for chefs and food enthusiasts. They come a long way to visit Rex Goldsmith and the boys at The Chelsea Fishmonger. Each morning his lively tweets herald the arrival of salmon from the Shetlands, shellfish from Scotland and an array of the freshest fish from Newlyn market and coastal waters. The selection and quality is of the highest standard, the jokes heading that way too. Two doors away, Andreas has opened a vegetable emporium with heirloom tomatoes and exotic mushrooms, bunches of fresh herbs and sun-ripened fruit. Tom Aikens continues to innovate and impress with his two restaurants. These three are pivotal to the growing swell of interest in the food available on Chelsea Green.

Elystan Street remains our only location. The temptation to open further shops has always been tempered by the reality that every new branch would sacrifice personal service and friendships with customers. In return Finns would become anonymous, our kitchens centralised and we would be a ubiquitous and faceless brand. As things are, our customers like our faces and we like theirs.

The early years of Finns were incredibly difficult and no-one is more surprised than me that this year marks our twenty-seventh on Chelsea Green. The pleasure it brings me now is largely due to the people who work there, their faces familiar to many, their stories less so. I thought their childhoods and the journeys which led them to Finns would interest the people who have come to know and rely upon them, as I do.

# Milly

When Finns was in its infancy, so too was Milly. The eldest of four siblings, she was brought up in Streatham in a large and rambling Victorian house. Her father was an insurance broker and her mother was a mother. Now twenty-eight, Milly grew-up with visits to Finns and as a young girl was setting up shops in her bedroom for the onslaught of imaginary customers to whom she sold home made sweets and cakes. I remember arriving for tea one cold February afternoon, beyond tired after a busy week at the shop and excited to be seeing my nieces and nephew. All quiet downstairs, Louise told me that Milly, eight, and Bella, six, were sunbathing in their bedroom. I walked upstairs to find the girls on colourful beach towels in Liberty bikini bottoms, sunglasses on, transistor radio between them blaring Flanders and Swann and a plate of freshly baked fairy cakes by their sides. Ever hospitable, Milly laid down a towel for me, Bella handed across the sun cream, and they shared out the cakes, blinded by the February sunshine.

Holidays were spent with grandparents in Yorkshire and Lancashire and long happy summers centred around the agricultural shows of Malham, Trawden, Gargrave and Rydal. Vast tents hosted bumper vegetables, enamel jugs with tall Dahlias usually grown by men, plates with five perfect eggs, Kilner jars of chutney and hedgerow jams all vying for the prizes in these highly competitive events in tents run by stern pillars of the Dales communities. Choosing the classes to enter with Granny Banny was as happy a time as any and the feverish crafting and baking which ensued produced many exhibits Finns would have been proud to sell. I remember a large straw hat which Milly decorated with shrunken crisp packets she had baked in the Aga to distorted colour foil squares, edible necklaces, cross-stitch bookmarks, rice crispie cakes and tray bakes – a chocolate brownie relatively alien to this pocket of rural England. On show days, a dainty Milly would be seen darting from produce tent to craft tent in her jodhpurs before being pulled away by a proud and highly competitive grandfather to win the handy pony competition.

I remember shooting weekends with Milly, Bella, Fred and Alice biking down to our cottage with dead pheasants over their handlebars, being implored to stroke the eye balls because they were "so silky." Milly would hunt with the Pendle Forest and Craven and many a hunt tea was eased by her willing and capable small hands as we strove to produce twenty-four perfectly cooked poached eggs and toasted crumpets simultaneously. This early foray into service has stood her in great stead when catering parties at Finns some twenty years on.

Her induction to the terrors of the till was courtesy of Granny Banny's Estate shop at Coniston where happy afternoons were spent on the shop floor rearranging produce, assembling hampers and enjoying the gentle patter of shop life.

When Milly was barely ten, her mother died. It was an extremely sad and difficult time not made easier by starting boarding school in York that September. The vision of a very petite and anxious Milly in her Mary Jane

shoes drowning in an oversized school coat brings a tear to my eye as I write. Queen Margaret's was, in the end, much beloved and the friends she made there remain loyal and true. In all the changing scenes of her life, Yorkshire and Lancashire have always been and still are her constants.

When Duncan, her father, remarried the family swelled with the addition of Tabitha, Mathew and Tom. A London allotment patch was a great diversion. Divided into six neat rows, the sibling rivalry flourished amongst the vegetables. Milly was adamant that family produce should continue to be exhibited. She grew prize marrows on the manure heap and lovingly tended her radishes to compete with the very best the North could produce. The entire Bowring gaggle were regularly loaded into the car, their Swiss rolls, carrot cakes and jam tarts balancing on their laps, their wares to be proudly displayed and red, yellow and white certificates eagerly sought.

After leaving school, Milly came to stay with us in London and embarked on a short work experience placement at Sotheby's where she was initiated not only in the art of photocopying but also the art of making coffee for large numbers. Her placement coincided with staff shortages at Finns and straight after Sotheby's a green pinny was donned and Milly got a taste of the ever hectic Christmas rush and an introduction to the many faces she now serves and talks to each day.

Just as I had been enthralled by the freedom and friendship I found in Oxford, so too did Milly love the life London afforded her. Emerging from Durham University, London beckoned once more. There was work as a PA, and then as a City Head Hunter. It was not the life for her. Seizing on her unsettled career, I lured her back to Finns where she had made such a mark and had been so happy. She has never looked back and Finns has never looked better.

# Katie

Katie grew up just seven miles from the Norfolk coast in the tiny village of Bale. Coming sixteen years after the youngest of her two older sisters, Katie was a delightful surprise to her parents. Her father runs a series of petrol stations in Norfolk and her mother is a mother. Her mother had previously worked in a bakery, cycling a basket full of bread around the village before devoting her time to her children, her household and her garden when she married. It is to Norfolk that Katie retreats at weekends to raid the garden for fruit and vegetables, bake cakes and bread on her mother's much used Aga, and to teach her young niece, Ellie, to be the chef she already knows she wants to be.

Amongst Katie's most treasured possessions is her late grandmother's diary in which extravagant and exquisite tea parties are recorded. Her mother's mother would make Eccles cakes, pancakes flavoured with brandy and studded with currants, lavender biscuits, breads and rose water sweets. These she would exchange for goods which passing travellers would proffer. For Katie this resourceful, generous nature is a continuing inspiration.

By thirteen, Katie was an impressive and ambitious cook. Unbeknownst to her parents, she applied to Junior Masterchef. It was only when she got through to the final stages of the competition that she revealed her secret.

One menu comprised of sea bass with a basil and pine nut puréed crust, griddled cherry tomatoes and a chervil sauce followed by marmalade ice-cream; another saw her craft a coffee cup out of brandy snap mixture and fill it with espresso ice-cream. Bale was replete with tales of her success and she featured both on the radio and in the local press.

After finishing school, Katie went to Cheltenham University and read Hotel Management and Hospitality. The first year involved no practical work and it was only during a second year placement in a hotel kitchen that she felt she was playing to her strengths. Her Head Chef was an obsessive exerciser and could often be found passed out in the pastry section. Much of the responsibility for running the kitchen fell to Katie and it is no coincidence that today she rises to the challenge in a crisis and leads the kitchen through the myriad different orders each day.

Before her arrival at Finns, she made her mark working for Anton Mossimann at the exclusive private members club off Belgrave Square. Starting at reception she quickly and quietly moved up into the events team eventually becoming the Guest Relations Manager. Her years at Mossimann's prepared her well for the demands of the busy summer months and Christmas rush at Finns. Ever organised, there is no crisis which cannot be sorted out with a good and structured list. Katie arrived at Finns within a week of Milly. She took over the responsibility of managing the kitchen leaving Milly to concentrate on managing the shop. In a short space of time, Finns gained two perfect new additions.

Livvie, Lizzie, Julia and Kevin. First food show, Bloomsbury, 1983.

Julia and Livvie, "Seafood '82," Boston USA.

*Good Housekeeping*, 1986.

Finns first postcard, 1986.

Louise Bowring and Julia. Birthright, Christmas 1986.

Nick Bannister, Tanya Ware, Julia,
Beth Stewart-Findlay, Tom Bannister.
Carols on the Green, 1989.

Beth and Tanya.

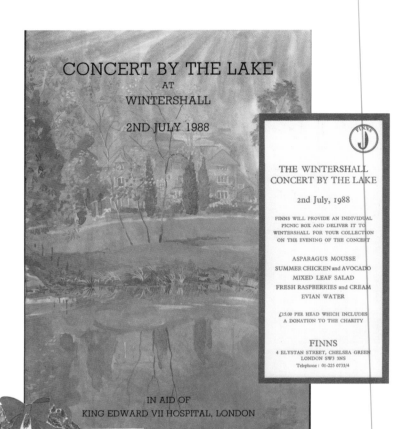

CONCERT BY THE LAKE
AT
WINTERSHALL

2ND JULY 1988

IN AID OF
KING EDWARD VII HOSPITAL, LONDON

THE WINTERSHALL
CONCERT BY THE LAKE

2nd July, 1988

FINNS WILL PROVIDE AN INDIVIDUAL
PICNIC BOX AND DELIVER IT TO
WINTERSHALL FOR YOUR COLLECTION
ON THE EVENING OF THE CONCERT

ASPARAGUS MOUSSE
SUMMER CHICKEN and AVOCADO
MIXED LEAF SALAD
FRESH RASPBERRIES and CREAM
EVIAN WATER

£15.00 PER HEAD WHICH INCLUDES
A DONATION TO THE CHARITY

FINNS
4 ELYSTAN STREET, CHELSEA GREEN
LONDON SW3 3NS
Telephone : 01-225 0733/4

Christmas
Dinner
18 December 1987

Smoked Salmon, Spinach Roulade with Smoked
Salmon & Cream Cheese & Watercress Roulade

Roast Goose stuffed with prunes & apricots.
Brussels Sprouts & Chestnuts. Spicy Red
Cabbage. Courgette, French Beans & Carrot

Chocolate Truffle Cake & Cream

English Cheeses. Biscuit. Salad
Tangerines. Nuts

Coffee & Mints

Champagne George Goulet. Muscadet.
Chateau Cordeillan. Armagnac. Port

Finns rocks with 184 picnics.

Finns catering at the Mall Galleries.

Decorating the shelves for Christmas, 1987.

Sonya Walger. Another busy day at Finns.

Mr Janson and friends.

# Chelsea Traders

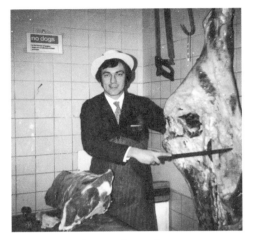

David Jago, the early years.

Rex at The Chelsea Fishmonger.

Tom Aikens
Photography: David Griffen
www.tomaikens.co.uk

Andreas

# Colette

Colette was born in Stanger, South Africa. Her father was a sugar cane farmer, as was her mother. Planted in tall rows, the leafy sugar cane plant is burnt before it is harvested. With her two brothers, Colette would race around her parents' farm lapping up raw sugar from the burnt crop or climbing the guava, mulberry, lemon, lime and mango trees which decorated their land. Her mother was a good cook and taught Colette how to prepare traditional South African dishes which, in turn, have found their way onto the Finns menu. Every Sunday, after church, Colette would snack on beef samosas before heading to the dam on the farm to make and sell mud pies to her mother, using the money to buy 'chappies' – tiny fruity sweets – from the local kiosk. Her summers were spent in Mauritius with her grandparents. Colette remembers drinking fresh mango juice which her grandmother made by squeezing ripe mangos until the flesh was a pulpy mass, puncturing the fruit's skin with a straw.

Inspired by her mother to become a chef, Colette attended The Silwood School of Cookery in Cape Town. Quite different to many of the cookery schools in the UK which cater for the aspiring chalet girl and accomplished newly wed, the three year South African diploma is designed for those wishing to have a career in top international catering kitchens. The students have to pay for all the ingredients they use and tough two month placements in some of Cape Town's busiest and best restaurants start during the second year. Her first placement saw her at the Mount Nelson, an exclusive hotel where she began to understand the pressures and requirements of working in a commercial kitchen. There followed time at the Beluga restaurant where she moved around each section, producing everything from complex starters to fine patisserie. This versatility serves her in great stead in the Finns kitchen. Before coming to England and to Finns, Colette spent her final two and a half years in South Africa working at 95 Keerom St. It was a new restaurant and when Colette went for her interview, it was little more than a building site. With just five other staff, she tested recipes, assembled menus and identified trustworthy suppliers. With such experience behind her, Colette's training and the training she gives to the new girls at Finns is second to none.

Colette moved to England in 2005 and started at Finns the following year. Having worked here for six years, she still relishes the freedom afforded by the Finns kitchen and that of working in a small team. In an environment in which everyone relies on everyone else, the bond between the girls is strong and it was being part of this unit of dedicated cooks which so appealed to Colette. As I talk to her about her childhood, she calmly scatters asparagus, courgettes and fennel over grilled salmon and talks to me about the 'braai,' the South African BBQ, which she is hosting tonight. Cooking is her lifeblood and her passion, it just so happens to be her job too.

# Marina

Marina was born on St Patrick's Day in the seaside town of Waterford, the oldest of Ireland's cities. Her father was a butcher and her mother a psychiatric nurse. The youngest of six siblings, Marina grew up in a large, noisy, culinary household where it was not uncommon to be given a sheep's eye with which to play, or take a trip *en famille* to the slaughterhouse with her father's cattle.

From a very young age, Marina was drawn to the kitchen, cooking and baking with her mother, brothers and sisters. The kitchen was a place to engage with the entire family, laughing and talking whilst preparing the dinners which were such a central part of each hardworking person's day.

The family collected the fruits and vegetables which could be found on their farm, eating with the seasons as much as possible and wasting little that the land gave them. Summers were spent foraging in the woods for mushrooms, six siblings all scrabbling around to find the biggest to take back to the kitchen and add to the tripe and onions which often graced the table. As August began, blackberries were sought and Marina would trot around the family farm on her pony, Rusty, who was as eager to find the fruit as she was.

Inspired by her sister who had attended Ballymaloe many years before her, Marina was first a student and then a teacher at Darina Allen's cookery school in Co. Cork. Like her childhood home, Ballymaloe is located on a farm. With such a background, Marina has a strong appreciation of natural produce. She admits that growing up and working in such environments was spoiling: it was only when she went to the United States in the 1990s that she realised eggs could come in a carton of six, a trip to the hen house always being her experience up until then. The ethos of Finns marks a continuation of her parents' attitude to food: where possible everything locally sourced, home grown and free range. At Finns, Marina feels she is the cook her mother inspired her to be: creative but careful, relying on natural ingredients with a strong desire to produce something good for someone else. Her mother, Marina tells me, views cooking as a survival skill. Marina is passing this mantra to her own daughter, Angel, as well as her mother's recipes for soda bread and Waterford's distinctive 'blaa' – a doughy, white bread roll. Cooking is Marina's past, her present and her future; it is her way of expressing herself and sharing in the lives of those she loves.

# Rosa

Rosa was born in Gloucestershire. Her father is a picture framer and her mother an interior designer. Her family home, an old mill, lies on the Coln river where she learnt to cast a line with her father from a young age. These early lessons sparked a passion for fishing and her holidays from Finns see her salmon fishing on the banks of the Naver or bonefishing on the sands of the Seychelles.

Like all the girls, Rosa grew up with a kitchen garden allowing her family to cook in tune with the seasons. As a child, her sister's Spanish godmother, Maria, cooked for the family just as she had done for Rosa's father when he was a boy. Maria's husband, Angelo, tended the garden and vegetables for lunches and dinners were gathered moments before they were needed. Rosa and her sisters would fight to pick the easily collected tomatoes, hiding only when asked to gather the strawberries, a task which involved grappling with netting, trapped birds and innumerable earwigs. She remembers the feasts Maria created from the garden's produce as well as the almost daily raids of the freezer for home made raspberry ice-cream.

Rosa embarked on her first cookery course during her final year at school, a five term programme run by Leith's School of Food and Wine. She loved it, from the first lesson of baking a Victoria sponge to the complex creation of three course dinners. The more she learnt, the more she wanted to learn. Newly graduated, Rosa drove herself to Co. Cork where she lived for three months and absorbed the fount of culinary expertise gifted by the teachers at Ballymaloe, just like Marina before her. Here, on the one hundred acre organic farm, was a way of cooking reminiscent of her childhood: from garden to kitchen to table, no food miles and little fuss.

After spending time working as a cook in both the Cotswolds and as 'a stage' at the London River Café, Rosa came to Finns. Having failed her first interview during which she nervously plunged pasta into a large pan of stone cold water, Rosa has listened to and learnt from her fellow cooks and it is with an uncompromising determination that she prepares delicious food each day. She draws inspiration from Maria, from Darina Allen, from those with whom she works and from the food of the countries she visits: from the small villages in Scotland to the street food in the colourful markets of Rajasthan.

With the introduction of the Finns café, the relationships with customers forged over the counter are as important to Rosa as the relationships she has forged in the kitchen. She has a warmth of character and genuine interest in the lives of others, as much a friend to those she works with as to those who come in to the shop.

# Marisa

Marisa was born one very cold winter in Ponte de Lima, a tiny market town on the South bank of the Lima river in the North of Portugal. A long medieval bridge connects Ponte de Lima to neighbouring Arcozelo and Marisa loves the little streets, the tumbling geraniums, the rich history and intense heat of one the oldest towns in Portugal.

Marisa's father was a carpenter and her mother was a mother. She is a wonderful cook and the traditional Portuguese dishes on which Marisa grew up are the same dishes she cooks each night for her husband and son, Joel. From her grandmother to her mother and then to Marisa, all the Dantas women follow the same recipes for dishes like cod bacalhau and beef casserola. For Marisa, to cook is to remember the years spent in her mother's and grandmother's kitchens, lapping up skills and licking the bowls. Cooking has always been a family business. Her grandmother and mother teamed together to create the wedding breakfasts for the lovers, young and old, in Ponte de Lima. Marisa and her four siblings would mimic their success by creating elaborate imaginary feasts in the living room, looking out onto the farm on which her grandparents grew everything from onions to be sweated in the casserola and sopa, to the grapes to be harvested for the family wine.

From a young age, Marisa was keen to make her own culinary mark and would wait for her grandmother to leave the house before raiding the cupboards for flour, sugar, butter and eggs, determined to make the definitive sponge cakes and pasteis de nata on which she had been raised.

Marisa moved to England when she was nineteen. She arrived at Victoria Coach Station speaking no English, with a photograph on top of her bag to identify herself to an agency which had promised her work.

After a lonely time and a succession of terrible jobs where she was mercilessly taken advantage of, she was referred to me by a family leaving Kensington for Hong Kong. She started working for my family in 2000 when Harry was six, Archie was five and Roddy just one. My children remember coming home from school to wonderful soups full of Portuguese pasta, roast chicken with soy and garlic potatoes, and handmade chips. She has kept an otherwise haphazard household in wonderful order, loved my children and been a tower of strength and quiet kindness whenever I have faltered. She and her family simply could not do more for me and mine.

With my children away at school, Marisa now turns her baking skills and perfectionism to the wafer thin Finns shortbread. Each piece carefully dipped in sugar, she cuts out chicks for Easter, angels, bells and stars for Christmas and hearts for Valentines' Day. Towards the end of each year, Marisa begins the task of crafting many thousands of mini mince pies for Finns' busy Christmas time, cutting out individual pastry stars to top each one. They are lovingly made and she embraces the numerous orders with pride.

It is only after talking to the girls about their childhoods and former jobs for this book that I realise I have never really read their CVs thoroughly. I tend to go on first impressions and for the main part I have been extremely lucky. The shop is now run by the strongest and most loyal team to date. After interviewing Marina she sent me a note. It read Thank You For Your Thyme. I thank her, and all the girls for their thyme too.

# The Story of Finns

We opened the doors of Finns on the 3rd October 1985, blinded by the glare of the stainless steel counters and a highly varnished, reconditioned oak floor. Modelled on the traiteurs and street markets of Paris and the gourmet food stores of New York, Finns set out to provide ready-cooked food from the small kitchen behind the shop. We had brought over a team of local builders from Kenmare who had never previously left the shores of Ireland. Taking their tools and their dust sheets, they boarded the freight ferry from Ringaskiddy to Barry Docks. We set them up in a B&B in Pimlico and became their interpreters and chauffeurs, ferrying materials from plumbing merchants and builders' yards to Finns each day.

Yellow walls layered with grease, inefficient fridges and vintage ovens together with an outside WC were all removed and replaced by gleaming worktops and modern kitchen equipment. Down one side of the shop the Irish builders built Welsh dresser style shelving under which we stacked our willow hampers. We painted everything bright white, save for the dark green logo hastily drawn on the back of an envelope with which to decorate our awning. At Christmas we put red insulating tape along the shelving edges, a 60p facelift for festive cheer.

Our plan was to fill the shelves so they overflowed with plenty. Our agenda was upset by the harsh reality of our finances: we simply had no money. I entered endless competitions to win ovens while we saved to buy commercial equipment. Our desks were £12 glossy trestle tables from Habitat still very much in use today. I don't remember if we had chairs, there was certainly no time to sit down.

For the first eighteen months, the day began at 5.30am at Billingsgate with wadges of cash, then on to Covent Garden by way of Smithfield, collecting our ingredients from each market. At Billingsgate the porters in their long white coats ferried our polystyrene boxes of wet fish and shellfish. At Smithfield, they loaded boxes of poussin, whole hams and cuts of lamb and beef. At Covent Garden, we loaded produce ourselves. It was physically tough, humping twenty kilo sacks of onions, carrots and potatoes only to be unloaded one hour later into the Finns kitchen. Exhausted we would start the day.

We did not sustain these foolish hours for very long and sought and experimented with different suppliers. In those days the telephone rarely rang with an order, only with the traders demanding their money and, as time went on, threatening court action. The bailiff left empty handed save an inventory of jams as we owned hardly any of the equipment. On a good day – a very good day – we would take £200 and with that sum would lure our suppliers to deliver the next morning, promising them their money on arrival. We had a bounty of small brown envelopes each containing £10 pinned to a board in the back office which we would give out to unsuspecting delivery men to await the wrath of their employers demanding the shortfall. We lurched from day to day and then from week to week, never entirely sure we would get to the end of the month.

Buoyed up by our bank manager's assurance that we would fail, we proceeded to sign every hire purchase agreement and personal guarantee that came our way. It was the first of two things my father forbade me ever to do, the second never to go into overdraft. As any small business owner will testify, signing a personal guarantee often becomes the only option when backed up against the wall. I, like thousands of other managers of start-up businesses, threw caution to the wind and became a co-guarantor to The City of Dublin Bank for our entire debt. Far more terrified of telling my father than being chased by the bank for the money which I did not have, this burden weighed very heavily on my increasingly skinny frame, which, under the stress of opening the shop, burnt calories at an extraordinary speed. My consumption of quiche, honey-baked sausages and salami and Emmental baguettes had, in those days, no bearing at all. Twenty-seven years and three children later, I long to recreate this 'diet' which required no willpower, no exercise and no abstinence of any kind.

We held a rainbow of credit cards which formed the basis of our 'working capital' but this was not enough. I remember a particularly grim Wednesday afternoon during which Livvie and I walked up and down Bond Street and through the Burlington Arcade trying to sell her jewellery. Everything, literally everything, had to go into the pot. We took no salary for the first five years and lived off the extensive choice of unsold food.

Thankfully, we had two things on our side: lots of importers and wholesalers were in their infancy and there were very few shops like Finns. This meant that, initially, people were very keen to supply us on our terms, delivering at times which suited us and sourcing products on demand. Unfortunately for the unwitting suppliers, our terms became more and more elastic to accommodate the overflow of unpaid invoices. To the bank managers, the importers and wholesalers alike, Kevin had one line: "We are doing our best." He had no fear of authority and memorably told the Inland Revenue that we would take our business elsewhere if they did not stop harassing and bullying us. He literally stormed the banks who queried our optimistic cash flow forecasts.

On the day we opened there was very little stock on the shelves. My mother produced a bumper crop of marmalade – thirteen jars – to which I added nine pots of herb jelly in three different flavours. We arranged these

jars very carefully and symmetrically, interspersed with fruit along the white shelves: lemon, space, orange, space, Jar, space, space, space, lemon, space, orange, space, Jar, and so on. Some seasoned retailer advised variety and height as the key to a good display, so we punctuated our jars and fruit with bottles of Perrier and Badoit, which we thought was the height of sophistication.

Livvie painted tall glass spaghetti jars and ceramic pots for paté and smoked fish butters. We filled the gaps with large china fish platters. There was equally little stock in the refrigerated counters. Fortunately *nouvelle cuisine* was the movement of the day so a little went a very long way. Rather beautiful white porcelain dishes hosted small pinwheels of roulade. Nine handmade Scotch eggs balanced like skittles in a bowling alley. Two large bowls of freshly made soup gave colour to a counter full of farmhouse cheeses, home made patés and olives. We baked baguettes and filled baskets with sandwiches. We soaked gammons in the back and sold baked ham on the bone; we offered smoked salmon hand sliced off the side and cut salami and bresaola on an oversized and unwieldy meat slicer. We drove to Rungis in Paris every month for fresh cheeses, walnut oils and organic wine.

In the beginning, we were more confident in the delivery of good service than we were in the fullness of our shelves. We wore a uniform of white shirts with large collars, long black skirts and rather impractical white aprons, which in retrospect looked somewhat Amish. We wrote all the labels by hand, never listed ingredients and measured the content by eye not scales. With no idea or formula of how to price anything we worked from gut feel rather than any form of margins. Anything ending in 99p was too obvious, as was 75p. I decided that all our prices would end in 6, 4 and 8. We thought that was unbelievably clever. We had no idea how to work the till or credit card machine but resolutely smiled our way through our incompetence.

Cheerfully returning one customer her card, we observed how clever to find a bank with the same name as her own. The customer looked up and smiled "The clever thing was marrying the man who owns the bank." Much to the amusement of the cashiers at Coutts today, we still use cloth money bags to deposit the weekly takings. These were phased out of circulation approximately eighteen years ago. In the early years we used to deposit the cash in the night safe on Sloane Square using a leather and brass pouch which resembled an over-sized sporran and invariably weighed more than the contents it held.

Our vision of serving queues of Chelsea residents did not materialise immediately. The initial reality was a daily average of eight sceptical customers, most of whom reassuringly told us that this shop was exactly what they did not want. One formidable customer disparagingly told us that all the food looked "D for disgusting." Whilst there was little competition, there was a definite resistance to buying home made food. We assuaged guilt, eased the lot of the time-poor career woman and reassured the newly burgeoning class of corporate wives. Feeling impotent having delegated us the catering, one customer enquired what else she could do to get ahead for the looming family party she was beginning to dread. We suggested, although it was still two days away, that she could always lay the table if that would make her feel better. The reply: "Darling, I did that two weeks ago."

Over time, customers took to the idea of bringing a dish for us to fill, plied us with cool boxes for their picnics and asked us to make cakes with burnt edges that had been volunteered for the home-baked school stall. One adventurous but somewhat suspicious octogenarian asked us to make salmon mousse, egg mousse and cucumber mousse and rang three times before collecting her order to ensure that we were not going to steal her three fine Herend porcelain dishes.

So with the confidence of our new customer base, one fateful Saturday soon after opening, we were left completely unprepared for the onslaught of what would now be termed 'foodies.' We had been interviewed the previous June by the highly respected Philippa Davenport, food journalist for the *Weekend Financial Times*. At the time of the interview, the dream had been to sell hand-raised game pies, home made fish soups, the best cooked sausages in London, our own potted shrimps and smoked fish patés. We worked out that the readers must have opened their *Weekend FT*, downed their freshly squeezed orange juice and roasted coffee and headed straight for Chelsea Green from as far afield as Henley and Hayward's Heath. By 4pm that day, 430 enthusiastic customers had come through our doors in eager pursuit of Philippa Davenport's recommended Dublin Bay prawns and hand-extruded sausages. We had none. In the blood, sweat and frequent tears of doing-up the shop we had long forgotten the interview and had never thought to check when it was going to appear. In one fell swoop, we almost lost all the goodwill that we had glimpsed.

From that Saturday to this I have religiously bought the *Weekend FT* in a silent tribute to that article. I have never since underestimated the impact of a small piece of editorial and made an early decision never to pay for advertising. For twenty-seven years, we have relied solely on word of mouth and praise of pen.

# A shop where they make a meal of it

**Philippa Davenport visits a new London food shop where many delicacies are created on the premises**

LONDON'S newest food shop, Finns of Chelsea Green, is a little different from most. What makes it unusual is that so many of the good things it sells are its own produce.

Most of its smoked and cured fish, poultry and pork products come from the Irish estate of one of the shop's owners, and these foods are supplemented by freshly-cooked dishes prepared in the kitchen at the back of the shop.

The "menu" will of course change daily but it should always include some soups, pates, marinades, salads, hot main course dishes and desserts. In other words, you can buy from Finns the wherewithal for a full-scale meal, so it could be a useful address to remember for days when you feel unwilling to cook and are not inclined to eat out in a restaurant.

Finns cure their own bacon and hams and smoke their own salmon, mackerel, luscious fat kippers, goose, chicken and turkey. They make their own sausages, and hand-raise pork and game pies.

They sell their own range of rich fish soups (95p per ½ litre), and pates, and lazy foods like mussels ready stuffed with garlic butter (£1.80 a dozen), miniature smoked salmon fish-cakes (45p each) and brochettes of mussels and bacon (75p each) ready to pop under the grill.

Meaty main course dishes to eat hot include spiced lamb with aubergines (£3.80 to serve four), individual steak and kidney puddings (65p), and pheasant with pate and mushrooms in port and cream sauce (£4.40 to serve four).

There are lighter dishes, including lovely sounding marinadet—gravadlax, carpaccio and Japanese-inspired ideas such as brill steeped in hazelnut oil with slices of pickled lemon and lime (from £2.20 to £2.50 per ¼-lb portion).

There are pasta sauces, sweet and savoury roulades, and cheeses (bought in) which include rarely-seen soft Italian varieties such as Robiola and Fiorone. Nice little extras include bunches of fresh herbs in season, home-made wholegrain honey mustard and garlicky apple jelly.

The foods are well turned out in terms of packaging. In fact some of the packaging is good enough to grace a dinner party table. For example, individual portions of smoked fish paté can be bought in tiny ceramic pots, which give the impression that the paté is yours rather than bought.

These ceramic dishes make the paté seem expensive initially (85p per portion) but the pots are refillable at the shop for 40p each.

Of all Finns' products, their Dublin Bay prawns excited me most. The prawns come fresh direct from the Irish estate, either split and stuffed with garlic butter, or plain.

Here is my recipe for the plain ones (which cost £4.20 per pound), a speedy and exceedingly greedy feast for two people:

**DUBLIN BAY SALAD**

Pull the heads off 2 lb whole raw Dublin Bay prawns. Split the tails along the soft underside, but do not shell them.

Grind pepper and salt over them, paint generously with best olive oil, and set aside for a few minutes while you put a loaf of bread to warm in the oven and lay a salad of lettuce and herbs (plenty of parsley and chives, and some mint or basil or dill) on a shallow serving dish.

Grill the prawns briefly, turning them as necessary and basting them with another good slurp of fruity olive oil. As soon as cooked, tip the prawns on to the salad and pour the pan juices over them.

Serve straight away with wedges of lemon and hot crusty bread.

Finns, 4 Elystan Street, Chelsea Green, SW3 (01-225 0733). Open Monday-Friday: 8 am-8 pm, Saturday: 8 am-1 pm.

*Financial Times*
Saturday 12 October 1985

Fernandes and his merry men.

A major event.

# Journey of a table cloth
# from Delhi to deli

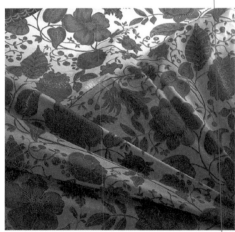

# Finns Gifts

Lydia distributing flyers.

Milly concentrating on the coffee.

The new coffee shop, August 2012.

# Finns Plates by Chelsea Artist, Ella Jackson

Katie

Julia

Colette and Rosa

Colette

# A Day in the Life

Eliza, Marisa, Rosa, Julia, Colette, Katie, Milly, Marina.

One of the customers brought in by Philippa Davenport's article was Mr Janson who proved to be one of the most loyal. For the last ten years of his life, he was an almost permanent presence in the shop, occupying a lone red chair next to the till. Daily he would regale us with different stories from Eton school days and his experiences in the army to his days with Shell. Each day, he would bring out a treasure or a trinket, an object to admire accompanied by the tale of its provenance. One day an engraved Georgian silver christening mug, another a correspondence he had had with the 11th Duke of Devonshire about town planning in Eastbourne. A first edition of Hillaire Belloc's *Cautionary Tales* followed a faded photograph of himself in an all in one bathing suit on the beach at Trouville. He made Finns the modern day equivalent of the 18th century coffee house owned by John Salter, situated a stone's throw away at 18 Cheyne Walk. Salter's coffee house was crammed with a melée of objects including a purse made of spiders from Antigua, a piece of Solomon's temple and a string of beads made from the bones of St Anthony.

Slowly but surely we won the confidence of other customers too and the order book was full most days. Despite our protestations, Kevin insisted we never said no. There was no concept of overtime. If we had to work through the night, we were lucky to have the business. However, unable to increase our payroll and employ enough people to staff the kitchen, the shop and the outside catering for which we were becoming increasingly in demand, Livvie and I waitressed every event. Flattered by the broad spectrum of catering demands, we became experts in floristry, sourced harpists and fiddlers, decorated cakes to any theme and lit fireworks when asked. In the early years, we often bit off more than we could comfortably chew but happily accepted the commission to cater for two West End musicals. Whilst Elaine Page as Grizabella was singing 'Memories' at the opening night of *Cats*, we were frantically filling ten kilo buckets with salmon and monkfish ceviche, kedgeree and other fish delights delivered at the eleventh hour during the interval to feed the Cats, the crew and their guests at their after show party. Likewise, while Fantine and Cosette sang of hunger and hardship in *Les Misérables*, we were similarly desperate to assemble a revolutionary feast for their opening night party.

In 1988, A Concert by the Lake at Wintershall saw us distribute one hundred and eighty-four individual picnic boxes filled with asparagus mousse, summer chicken with avocado and raspberries and cream, whilst Gary Brooker, Eric Clapton, Phil Collins, Mike Rutherford and Andy Fairweather Low entertained friends and fans alike.

The catering side of the business grew rapidly. Orders came in for picnics for the Grange, Garsington and Glyndebourne; the Fourth of June, Speeches and Sports Days; Lords, Twickenham, Ascot and Goodwood; casseroles and crumbles for weekend shoots, jellies and fairy cakes for children's tea parties. There were christenings, birthdays, anniversaries and wakes and, most harrowing of all, a funeral in Kensington of a Lockerbie bomb victim.

Despite the increasing demand inside the shop and out, we were dogged by cash flow problems, high interest rates, bank charges and a nation in recession. Cracks in the system began to appear and with too many cooks spoiling the broth, five years in, I left for six months and fled to Rome.

There I rented a charming garden flat, once lived in by Claudia Cardinale, on the Vicolo degli Orsoline next to the Santa Cecilia Music Academy below the Spanish Steps. I was very lucky to be taken on by Charles FitzRoy in the early years of Fine Art Travel and found myself assisting him and Peter Lauritzen with a tour group of trustees and friends of the Isabella Stuart Gardner Museum in Boston. They had come to Italy to see the splendours of Baroque Rome, to enter doors and palazzi not normally open to the public but to which Fine Art Travel was the key. My spare time was spent in the Campo dei Fiori market with its hustle and bustle of busy traders, where colourful stalls overflowed with fresh fish, festoons of sausages, salamis, prosciutto, vegetables, cheeses and truffles. Roman housewives, cooks, chefs, students on *Vespas* and bicycles and nuns in long robes squeezed and pinched, smelled and tasted the fiori di zucca, carciofi and Romanesco cauliflowers, filling their baskets as laughter and shouting filled the square.

I started each morning in the local Café Vittorio amongst familiar faces with a small machiatto and a panini served by a tall, dark and handsome Italian barista, Massimo. The Café Vittorio became my refuge from the demands of the terrifying tour and was never far from my thoughts when designing the new café at Finns. I hoped to mimic its atmosphere and pace, its feel and flow.

I travelled all over Tuscany and Umbria, reading Frances Mayes *Under the Tuscan Sun* and living on a diet of grated carrot, caraway seeds and mortadella. I arrived in Siena for the Palio where I bought a set of beautiful hand painted plates from a small studio in the labyrinth streets off the Campo. These plates formed the start of a collection of ceramics that has grown over the ensuing fifteen years. We use them for the photographs on our website and I use them for the chaotic dinner parties I cobble together at home.

Two months later, Serenissima Travel lured me to Leningrad where blinded by gold leaf I steered two tours through the Romanov palaces and eight inches of snow. Beneath the bridges over the Neva, we bartered packets of tea, cigarettes and lipstick in exchange for tins of caviar, real rabbit fur hats and T-shirts with the face of Gorbachev and *Glasnost* and *Perestroika* printed large. The quiet cold streets of Leningrad in those last days of Communist Russia were empty of shoppers. In the market, the trestle tables with torn fablon covers hosted small quantities of potatoes, leeks and onions sold by dour Russian babushkas in drab wool shawls and big grey gloves – a stark contrast to the noise and vibrancy of the Campo dei Fiori and the *dolce vita* of Rome.

After six months, I returned to England hardly rested but much refreshed. It was decided that the Coopers would sell me their half of the business and with a new energy, I picked up both reins and took up where I had left off. I changed banks, rebuilt relationships with scattered suppliers, and employed an agency called Success after Sixty to supply me with a book-keeper. I chose the only applicant, Rosamund. Built like Brunhilda and with a baritone voice to match, she radiated calm and good sense, allaying the many fears I had as the now sole owner. Armed with pencils and rubbers and an embroidered pouch of coloured biros, she rarely used the vast calculator with yellowing paper rolls, preferring to add her numerous columns by head and enter her debit and credit ledgers by hand. She swore at her rubber, cursed her totals, read Keats in her coffee breaks and trained me to keep the books as carefully as she had done. It was a sad day when she left to enter a retirement home run by Spanish Catholic nuns.

Again, I found myself working in the kitchen and shop six days a week. I missed Livvie dreadfully, the laughter which had carried us through was more often than not absent. It became essential in every respect to fill the gap with friends and family.

Always short-staffed on a Saturday, I regularly dragooned my family to come to the rescue, in particular my sister, Catherine, and my new sister-in-law, Louise. Unable to serve in the shop, Catherine's only brief with rapidly emptying fridges was to "Just Make More." I remember one infamous

Saturday with Catherine in the kitchen whizzing soups and rolling pastry, and Louise on the shop floor with the now more frequent queue of customers making a run on the baskets of *moules farcies* which had become such a success. Despite having told Louise that all mussel baskets were in the freezer, with depleted stock and an eagerness for a sale, she sold the display bourriche, a basket stuffed mainly with newspaper and mussel shells, a token few week old mussels piped with garlic butter balancing atop. We awaited the call from an irate customer but panic turned to dread as an ominous silence left us imagining the worst.

As the team expanded, the early days saw me struggling to describe the job vacancy for a six centimetre advertisment in *The Lady*. The recession of the late eighties and early nineties saw applications from all walks of life: old and young, male and female, those prepared to relocate and start lives in an unfamiliar city. I include two replies to our advertisement during these early years, so very different from anything we receive today.

I remember too interviewing a twin from a large family who, at her trial, was capable, confident and charming. Three days into her job her cooking lacked assurance and competence and her character lacked the vivacity and grace she had displayed at her trial. I further noticed her arm lacked the large mole she had revealed at her interview. When tentatively challenged, it became apparent that she was the other twin whose sister did all the interviews and trials on her behalf. I let her go, marvelling at their combined boldness.

We employed one very pretty, strawberry blonde from Hartlepool. Newly arrived in London, she had always "fancied working in Chelsea." She confessed to being totally disinterested in food, had no wish to learn how to cook but liked talking to people. Tempted by her extremely neat and tidy appearance, engaging manner and enthusiasm to work solely in the shop, I struggled to balance her redeeming qualities with her fundamentally unenthusiastic attitude to food. I decided to call her back for a second interview and that the most important thing to establish was whether she had a good sense of humour. When I asked the following question "Are you funny?". She replied "No! I thought I told you, I have a boyfriend." She was instantly hired, became a favourite of many, but left two years later when the boyfriend became the husband and they went to live in California.

<u>C U R R I C U L U M   V I T A E</u>

Date of Birth: 30<u>th</u> April, 1950.
Marital Status: Single.
General Health: Moderately Good.

EDUCATION
Sept.1961 to June 1966. Upton House Comprehensive School, LONDON,E.9.left aged 16 with 'O'level
G.C.E. Music and Religion. C.S.E. Gr.1. Geography,Gr.2. English and Mathematics.
STUDY AND TRAINING
Jan. to June 1973. BATH Tech.Coll.Dept.of Emp.,Commercial Course – Cetificate and 4 'O'levels
plus R.S.A.Typewriting.
1975 to 1976. Evening Classes CHELMSFORD C.F.E. 'A'level G.C.E. English(E) Sociology (B).
1986 to 1987. Full Time FRAINTREE C.F.E. City & Guilds Catering 706/1 with credits.
1987 to 1989. Own Time, a day a week, CHELMSFORD I.H.E. then C.F.E., R.I.P.H.H.cert pass 88,
City & Guilds Catering 706/2 Distinction and credits 89.
WORK HISTORY

| | |
|---|---|
| 7-66 to 10-66Berkeley Hotel LON.W.1. Kitchens | 8-69 to 2-70 Bridge Home WITHAM,Laundryman |
| 11-66 to 1-67 Co-op Chemists LON.E.15 Counters | 4-70 to 9-70 David Hicks LON. SW3. Servant |
| 4-67 to 1-68 H.Lait Furniture WITHAM,Labourer | 11-70 to 3-71 Margail Plastics WITHAM, Kilnwork |
| 2-68 to 6-68 Co-op E.15 as before | 5-71 to 8-71 Pontins Brean SOMERSET,Hols.Kitchens |
| 7-68 to 1-69 Hackney Hosp,LON.E9 Ward Orderly | 8-71 to 10-71 Wellworthys SOMERSET,Lathes |
| 1-69 to 2-69 Stationers E.2,Office Work | 5-72 to 6-72 Ross Poultry TROWBRIDGE,Grader |
| 3-69 to 4-69 Hosp,E.9. as before | 7-72 to 9-72 Co-op Retail BATH, Liftman |
| 4-69 to 6-69 Typesetters EC1 Telephone Copy | |
| 7-69 to 8-69 Grollier Books Europe U.S.Bases Direct Sales | |

7-73 to 11-74 D.H.S.S. Pensions Clerk, BATH       2-78 to 3-78 Alfred Marks,Temp Clerk,LON.
10-74 to 7-76 Marconi Purchasing Clerk,CHELMSFORD 6-78 to 7-78 Urch Harris, Stamp Packing,BRISTOL
8-76 to 11-77 Federal Elect,Int,Inc.Stock Clerk  7-79 to 12-79 W.Weddel,Stats.Clerk,LON,EC1.
Germany then Italy on U.S.Bases

2-80 to 1-81 Doe Motors WITHAM, Cleaner, Left for aborted computers course.
7-81 to 4-82 Westcliff Hotel SOUTHEND,Hall Porter while Studying to be Butler,Left for Interviews
11-82 to 5-83 R.Fuhrer LON,W1. Butler (Cooking,Wine,Silver,Cleaning...)Sacked in Employers Pique
8-83 to 7-84 Mr Stopford Sackville NORTHAMPTONSHIRE,Under Butler (Fires,Cleaning,Security,Table,
little driving)Left when other staff but Me gone months twice over,roof fell in, My car crashed
on Estate Police refusing to attend,window blew in.
7-85 to 10-85 Nadell Patisserie LON,N.1. Beginner Pastry Cook. Money not viable.
7-87 to 6-90 Bridgemarsh CHELMSFORD, Cook in Charge,(Cooking,Cleaning,Orders,Stores for 40 Retarde
and Staff)Left for less Emotionally demanding Job and to meet new Tax Charges.
6-90 to 7-90 Post Office Quadrant Caterers, CHELMSFORD,Night Cook. Left through Low Pay and
defemation plus gross Hygiene lapses of Employers.
To Present Unemployed. Some Temp Cooking Jobs Done, I Clean Church Hall 6 Hrs a week.
SPARE TIME ACTIVITIES
Attend Church of England, Recently Joined international Penfirends club,Read, Study, try to
follow Art, Music, Literature(Poetry). I do Charity stalls, invent sweets,am friend of Museums.

ADDITIONAL INFORMATION. I stopped smoking in 1988,cycle(not racer) live quietly with old and
ill Parents, have money worries and burdens so am not immediately usefull for a leading of
people position. But I have hopes.

## EXPERIENCE

**HARROGATE AGENCY    HARROGATE**                                          1987 – 89
Relief Chef
* Employed by an employment agency, relieving chefs who were on holiday leave or sick
* Expected to be able to take any chef role up to head chef
* Responsible for all kitchen staff as head chef and for ensuring the smooth and efficient running of the kitchen
* Required to be flexible enough to work in a variety of establishments from top hotel to bistro to rest home to restaurant

**GARDEN MERCHANTS (CLEANING CONTRACTORS)   UNICEP BARRACKS**
**HARROGATE**                                                              1987
Chargehand Cleaner
* Responsible for a staff of 12 cleaners and for delegating work to same
* Ensured that cleanliness of kitchen and dining rooms was maintained to a high standard
* Polished floors daily and used domestic cleaning equipment

**HORNBEAM COLLEGE**                                                       1986 – 87
Student
* During this period was engaged on a City & Guilds Course in Catering 7061/7062

                              **SPALDING**                                 1985
Slaughterman
X* Removed heads from pigs which were on a conveyor belt
* Cut carcasses into large pieces which were then butchered into joints etc.
* Removed giblets from animals

**MOAT HOUSE   PRESTON**                                                   1984
Wine Waiter/Silver Service Waiter   (Days)
* Acted as a wine waiter, advising customers on best selection
* Worked as a Silver Service Waiter ensuring an efficient service

**PEPPERMINT PLACE**                                                       1984
Doorman/Barman   (Evenings)
* During the week, worked as a barman, serving customers with beer, wine and spirits etc. in a pleasant and efficient manner
* Stocked bar and handled cash ensuring that the correct change was given
* Responsible for tidying the cellar and changing barrels and took deliveries
* At weekend, employed as a doorman

**PETRA MCNAUGHT (METAL WORKS)   ROCHDALE**                                1980 – 83
Furnaceman
X* Broke cast iron into manageable pieces using a lump hammer
* Placed iron pieces into barrow for transportation to the top of the furnace
* When melted, the iron was poured into moulds
* After 24 hours, when set, the moulds were emptied and casting was cleaned and removed for transport

**MINKEY CLOTHS   ROCHDALE**                                              1979
Stock Controller
* Took delivery of rolls of cloths
* Delivered cloth to machinists
* After packaging, brought cloths to stores area
* Loaded wagons with finished goods ensuring paperwork was completed satisfactorily

**J. & J. MAKIN   (PAPER)**                                               1975 – 78
Stock Control/Fork-Lift Driver

**BESWICK PICKLES   ROCHDALE**                                            1972 – 74
Stock Controller
* Engaged in stock control in similar work to that at Minkey Cloths

## EDUCATION & TRAINING

Balderstone Grammar School, Rochdale                                      1967 – 72

Hornbeam Park College                                                     1986 – 87
     City & Guilds Catering 7061 & 7062

## PERSONAL DETAILS

     Date of Birth:      12.12.56
     Marital Status:     Divorced
     Health:             Excellent

## ACTIVITIES & INTERESTS

     Fishing
     Swimming
     Walking
X    Camping and Survival
     Creating Vegetable Menus
     Food Preparation

I received a letter from a sixteen year old asking for a job during the Christmas holidays. I telephoned her and suggested she send her CV listing her Name, Date of Birth, School, Qualifications and Interests. I received by return a five line CV:

For many years we subcontracted our waitresses and butler requirements to an agency. We gave them a strict dress code: black skirt, white blouse with a collar, clean shoes, hair back, no jewellery, no nail varnish. I thought the rules were pretty black and white, but apparently not. One girl arrived in Ugg boots, laddered tights and a black armband. Horrified, I tried, at least, to get rid of the latter. Impossible: it was a tattoo. It was not the most exotic body art I have seen on the payroll. We have had the map of Italy on a lower back, including Sicily, Porto Ercole and Giglio. I finally did away with the agency when they sent me an Australian girl in a grey T-shirt, bare hairy legs and a black skirt scrumpled up in a plastic bag, planning to ask the hostess to set-up an ironing board.

In the end, Katie and Colette wanted the customers to take comfort from the fact that those who made their food would be serving their food and they insisted that we find a dedicated team of butlers to support them. It was determined that if we could not staff the event ourselves, we should not undertake it. In the back of an old diary, I found the telephone number of Herculano Fernandes, a most excellent Portuguese butler who had helped at some of our earliest functions. I gave him the task of building a team of highly professional, immaculately dressed and consistently punctual waiters. Martin, Antonio, Armandio and Avilio are now available to Finns on demand and our happy partnership with Fernandes and them has flourished ever since.

With increasingly high overheads, I looked for a way to give the business another dimension. It seemed a natural extension to include a range of gifts that complimented the food we sold. Customers regularly sought to borrow our dishes and their busy lives which ensured their custom often meant that the borrowed dishes were never returned. With the Euro in our favour, I began to import ceramic dishes from Provence which customers could buy as presents as well as leaving with us to fill. The success of these dishes led to a range of bespoke table cloths, table mats, trays, candlesticks and glass which Milly with her fresh eyes, good taste and sense of style has expanded since her arrival at Finns.

Our eclectic range of customers share our taste and buy gifts and presents to decorate their houses and delight their friends. The demand for an ever-changing variety of products that would be unique to Finns led us on one memorable trip from our deli to Delhi to the Residence of the then British High Commissioner, Sir Richard Stagg. No sooner had we drawn up at the Lutyens designed Residence at 2 Rajaji Marg and unpacked with a *nimbu pani*, were we ushered into a party in honour of the Queen's birthday. Milly and I moved amongst two thousand representatives of other British firms. It was the beginning of a wonderful week on a trip to source individual and distinctive gifts to brighten the shelves at Finns during which we were astounded by the colours, sights, smells and noises of India. Arabella Stagg steered and guided us through the busy markets, setting up meetings for us in Uttar Pradesh and Jaipur, helping us find suitable manufacturers to produce hand-blocked cotton table cloths and hand-painted ceramic dishes, lanterns and enamel teaspoons. Weeks after our return huge brown parcels began to arrive, their highly eccentric outer packaging and often unexpected contents bringing different surprises to our small corner of Chelsea. Upon our return, a dashing nonagenarian admired the earrings I had bought in India. On hearing I had been introduced to a brilliant one-eyed jeweller in Delhi who could copy or design any piece, he asked me to get something made for his wife to whom he was utterly devoted. I asked what she would like and suggested he get a photograph of something I could have copied. His reply "She likes cardigans. How about a dozen decent diamonds with rubies and emeralds with which she can replace her buttons – whatever you think, dear, I leave it to you."

This same dashing nonagenarian ordered his entire Thanksgiving feast from us each year. Undaunted by the weight of a 22lb turkey, stuffed, trussed and oven ready on a roasting tray, he sent his housekeeper and her husband with his wife's wheelchair. There followed a procession from Finns with two retainers wheeling the chair along the pavement resplendent with turkey atop a large cushion and an extended retinue of Finns girls carrying creamed onions, parsnip purée, pecan and pumpkin pies.

Thanksgiving is our busiest Thursday in the year with many Americans bringing in their oven trays for turkeys and flan dishes for pies. All staff are booked far in advance of this gourmet celebration. As December approaches, we share stories of the different traditions and celebrations with our Spanish, French, Italian and Russian customers. Many who come to live in Chelsea seek to know how to celebrate a truly English Christmas and we enjoy explaining about sixpences hidden in the Christmas pudding and kissing under the mistletoe.

A year ago, twenty-seven years after its initial refurbishment, Finns closed for a month. For many years our customers had implored us to serve really good quality coffee and urged us to create a little area where they could sit and eat the food produced each day. Given the confines of an already small shop, we took on the excellent Simon Colley of Cooper 8 to design a new layout both for the shop front and the kitchen behind. His brief was to incorporate a seating area and coffee bar whilst retaining the feel and familiarity of the original Finns. The dresser was made slimmer, the refrigerated cabinets custom built, the baker's rack banished upstairs and a coffee bar built in the corner. The sole chair once nearly always occupied by Mr Janson, was replaced by four small round tables and twelve chairs. Within the large window overlooking the small stretch of grass we installed a narrow bar and five stools – a popular haunt for those wishing to watch the comings and goings on the Green.

Soon after the refurbishment, Lydia Owen Edmunds came to Finns ready for a short diversion from the high and low notes of life as a singer songwriter. She designed a tempting voucher and armed with her Oxford degree, essential, she eagerly embraced the challenge of pounding the pavements around Chelsea Green. With a spring in her step and a large smile on her face, she distributed vouchers for free coffee and dispensed Finns stickers to bemused children. Joined by her brother, Casimir, on the ukulele, these merry minstrels attracted queues of coffee drinkers to our newly opened café. Many have been regulars ever since.

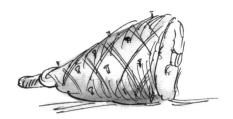

# Today

Twenty-seven years after we opened our doors, whilst a day in the life of Finns can be full of surprises, the rhythm and routine stays largely the same. First thing in the morning as Chelsea Green awakens, Rex the Fishmonger sets out his stall, Jago the Butcher unloads his van of fresh meat and Geoff the window cleaner fills his bucket. The Finns cooks arrive early, parking their bikes against the railings. Ovens ON, air-conditioning ON, refrigerated display cabinets ON, coffee machine ON, thermometers CHECK. The awning down, the day begins. The chefs' whites are donned, ready to greet the suppliers. First come Ravi and Deepak with the vegetables, then Big John and Little John from the butchers on Elystan Street followed by Dominick the Buffalo Mozzarella Man and other Wise Men bearing their produce to the kitchen behind the shop. The deliveries are checked and stored in the walk-in chill room.

From upstairs, bucket loads of pulses, flour, dried fruit and nuts are carried down. The order book is full and within half an hour all eight oven rings are glowing and all ten oven shelves groaning with herbed chicken breasts, honey-mustard sausages, marinated cod, roasting vegetables, and whole gammons studded with cloves. Marina's bread snuggles close by on a shelf proving in the warmth, waiting its turn in the oven. Marisa sets up her sandwich station. Knives are chosen, and a mosaic of coloured chopping boards laid over the stainless steel tables. Vegetables are scrubbed and herbs chopped; blenders whirr and whisks clatter. There is half an hour to set the wheels in motion before the doors are opened. It is a precious half hour and every minute is valuable.

The doors open and the regular customers call by. They drop off dishes from home to be filled with casseroles, kedgeree and pies to be collected later in the day or week. They sit down for a quick coffee and regale the girls with tales of a rumoured tenant for the empty shop across the Green, the fire which closed the King's Road, the exhibition at the Saatchi Gallery and the cocktail party at the Chelsea Physic Garden. The easy manner with which Milly creates our signature dark bourbon roast coffee belies the skill required to make each cup. Each morning, she opens a new bag of shiny, dark coffee beans which are ground on demand throughout the day. A paintbrush sweeps the group handle clean before fourteen grams of coffee are tamped down to produce a smooth black surface. She replaces the handle to the espresso machine and not-quite-boiling water drips through the coffee into small glass tumblers to produce the perfect crèma which provides the base for all good espresso. This process should take twenty-five seconds but the time alters depending on the heat of the shop and the moisture in the air. With a discrete stopwatch, Milly keeps her eye on the timer and adjusts the gauge of the coffee grinder throughout the day. She warms a white coffee cup and pours in the espresso. The milk is gently steamed, the jug swirled and banged to create a glossy texture for the latte or frothy mass for the cappuccino. With an inimitable flick of the wrist, Milly pours milk over the espresso to create highly original and bespoke latte art served with a smile.

The daily menu is written up and emailed to local shops and offices. Marisa lines up seven mugs and fills them with milky coffee. Marina takes her quiches out of the oven and the smell of cheese and bacon wafts through to the shop. Soups and salads fill bags, patés and hummus are seized on, muesli and fruit compôte bought for the diet that starts tomorrow and carrot cake resisted. Amidst it all a delivery of cloth carrier bags arrives from China via Lancashire: a vast lorry clogs the narrow Chelsea streets. Oblivious to the hooting horns, a cheerful delivery man drops a vast pallet in the narrow shop doorway. There's nothing for it – it's all hands on deck, customers included, to unload the boxes. The traffic must flow, not just on the street. A second supplier with fluorescent pink hair arrives from East Anglia. On leaving she asks for a piece of old toast or an oatcake – any little scrap for the chickens she has left in her car outside. As we look on in amazement, we are reassured "Don't worry, my girls adore London."

Milly and Rosa steal a moment from the ringing shop tills to drink their coffee in the kitchen: it is cold. Marisa pours seven cups of coffee down the sink and starts again. The telephone continues to ring. Someone is having a dinner in a week's time. They've caught a salmon; can we make hollandaise? A group of friends have decided to forgo the restaurant after the theatre: are we making risotto or fish pie? A dinner for twenty looms for the nervous hostess: can she have Fernandes and his merry men to help serve the drinks and Katie and Colette to serve the food? How many canapés should she order? Should she serve cheese before pudding? Can we deliver?

Rosa starts to carve the ham for the lady with the pram. As she hands over the carrier bag and goes round to admire the baby, she tries to disguise her surprise. It is a dog. A large 4x4 draws up with a honking horn demanding attention. The immaculate housewife all but frisbees her lasagne dish into Rosa's expectant arms and accelerates away.

The tables begin to fill and the conversation flows. Customers proudly show off photographs of their new grandchildren, tell tales of the last puppy sold, the pony put down, the success of the opening night; they ponder over crosswords, immerse themselves in newspaper and novel, discuss their wardrobes and their share portfolios. Late morning sees Colette, Katie, Marina and Rosa bearing four large pots with hot soup and the hot dish of the day: spiced butternut squash or watercress and courgette soup, minted lamb casserole with mashed potatoes or prawn egg fried rice with sweet chilli and ginger. Two Australians sit at the window bar and decree their flat whites the best since they left Sydney. Local office workers and traders alike come for a few moments away from desk and till. Regular customers meet friends for lunch and queues form whilst they gently argue and firmly insist to foot the bill. Should somebody famous cross the threshold, rather than squeal with unbridled excitement, the girls shout through to the kitchen to take the COD out of the oven. This is our private and subtle signal for a casual walk through the shop to view the Celebrity On Display. Tired shoppers sit down to restorative herbal teas, small children do their homework spurred on by a chocolate brownie and a glass of lemon cordial, taxi drivers and envoys collect the orders for the evening, Marisa irons the waitresses shirts upstairs and Fernandes arrives to load the canapés for a cocktail party. Distractions and diversions throughout the day see 6pm come very quickly. Ovens OFF, air-conditioning OFF, refrigerated display cabinets emptied, coffee machine cleaned and OFF, thermometers CHECK. Awning up, lights off, the day ends.

We have twenty-seven past diaries, heavy black books with pages and pages of orders. They chart the journey of this business and are a treasured record of the day-to-day comings and goings of the people who shop at Finns. Actors, actresses, authors, playwrights, cabinet ministers, models, Catholic priests, rock stars, Royals from home and abroad, one Sixties fashion icon and one Wimbledon champion. Fathers and sons, mothers and daughters, we thank you all.

# Notes on the Recipes

The recipes which follow have been introduced and developed by the girls who have worked at Finns and inspired and modified by the customers who have supported us.

The nature of Finns means that the majority of our dishes are prepared in advance and devised to be reheated. As such, the following recipes are good for cooks who wish to get ahead; they make for stress free dinner parties during which you do not have to fly off to the kitchen and abandon your guests. We recommend cooking all fish and searing all meat the morning before your guests arrive. In this way, any fishy smells and smoke will have long since dissipated.

The provenance of our ingredients is extremely important to us and those we use are fresh, mainly from the British Isles and always of the highest quality. Our meats, poultry and fish are free range and organic where possible. All eggs are free range and large, unless otherwise stated. Fruits and vegetables are fresh, with the exception of baby broad beans, edamame beans and peas. Herbs are always fresh and any parsley we use is Italian flat leaf.

Ingredients, particularly fruit and vegetables, will vary in taste throughout the year. We urge you to taste your cooking regularly and adjust your seasoning accordingly.

All meats, vegetables, and eggs start at room temperature unless specifically stated otherwise.

We use stem ginger paste in a number of recipes. For this, we buy best quality stem ginger in syrup, blend the whole jar with a hand stick blender and return it to the same jar. It can then be kept in the fridge for up to a month and used in many different recipes.

The pans we use are good quality and heavy based. These make for a more even cooking and help prevent the burning of meat, delicate vegetables and butter based sauces. All our cooking temperatures are based on a fan oven but every oven is different so cooking times may have to be adjusted slightly.

Although there is a movement towards using British rapeseed oil in dressings and general cooking, its flavour is very distinctive and not to everybody's taste. We find that a light olive oil or vegetable oil works very well for general frying and cooking and have stated the best choice for each individual recipe. However, a good quality extra virgin olive oil is essential for dressings, sauces and finishing dishes.

# Soups

*Soup is as old as the art of cooking.*
*In fact, it goes back to the ages before cooking was an art at all.*
BETTY CROCKER

Courgette and Watercress
Roasted Tomato and Basil
Chunky Chicken Noodle
Spicy Butternut Squash
Cucumber and Mint
Asparagus Vichyssoise

Each time I make soup, I think of my grandmother and the busy kitchen of her small house in Oxford where I stayed every Wednesday for three happy years. She shopped at Oxpens market, carrying vegetables in the basket of her bicycle, 'Gigi.' She was still cycling around the streets of Oxford in her nineties. She called her soups SOS: Soup Of Sorts and they were filled with left over vegetables and meats from a week of lunches and suppers. Made with home made vegetable stock, they were as delicious as they were varied. For the recipes below, home made stock has been listed as an ingredient. The recipes for vegetable, chicken and beef stock can be found on pages 98–100. Using the best quality stock cube available is a fine substitute but beware the addition of too much salt.

# COURGETTE & WATERCRESS
## for 8

This is one of our most popular soups in the shop. Regularly ordered, it works well hot and cold and is an all year round favourite.

Ingredients

9 large courgettes, cut into 1 inch slices
250g watercress
1 large onion, diced
2 litres vegetable stock (p.98)
olive oil
salt and freshly ground black pepper

Method

In a large heavy based saucepan with a lid, sweat the onion in a little olive oil on a low heat for about 10 minutes until soft and translucent.
Add the courgettes and stock and bring to the boil.
Simmer for 25 minutes or until the vegetables are soft, placing a lid on the saucepan.
Remove from the heat before stirring in the watercress.
Blend with a hand stick blender until smooth.
Season to taste.

# ROASTED TOMATO & BASIL
## for 8

This soup is delicious in summer or winter. In the summer, add a dollop of mascarpone to each bowl and sprinkle with some freshly torn basil. In winter, drizzle with a little pesto or scatter with home made croûtons. If you struggle to find good, ripe tomatoes, 2 cans of best quality tinned tomatoes can be used as a substitute. Add 1 teaspoon of caster sugar for each tin to replicate the sweetness of fresh ones.

Ingredients

1 large onion, diced
1 clove garlic, crushed
12 large ripe tomatoes
2 litres vegetable stock (p.98)
large handful fresh basil, finely chopped
olive oil
extra virgin olive oil
salt and freshly ground black pepper

Method

Preheat the oven to 180°C.
Slice the tomatoes in half, remove their cores and place on a roasting tray. Drizzle with extra virgin olive oil, salt and freshly ground black pepper and roast for 45 minutes.
In a large heavy based saucepan, sweat the onion in a little olive oil for about 10 minutes on a low heat until soft and translucent.
Add the garlic and sweat for a further 2 minutes.
Add the roasted tomatoes, vegetable stock and basil. Bring to the boil before turning down the heat and allowing to simmer for 40 minutes.
Remove from the heat.
Blend with a hand stick blender until smooth.
Season to taste.

# CHUNKY CHICKEN NOODLE
for 6 – as a hearty lunch

This hearty, filling soup is perfect for autumnal lunches. We usually use a whole cooked chicken, the roasting producing such great flavours. Whilst thyme and marjoram work well, rosemary, lemon thyme and oregano can be substituted. Any leftover soup will freeze very well.

Ingredients

300g cooked shredded chicken
2 litres chicken stock (p.99)
80g egg noodles, broken into small pieces
1 medium onion, finely diced
2 medium carrots, finely diced
4 medium celery stalks, finely diced
1 teaspoon fresh thyme leaves
1 teaspoon fresh marjoram
olive oil
salt and freshly ground black pepper

Method

In a large heavy based saucepan, sweat the finely diced vegetables in a little olive oil on a low heat for about 10 minutes until soft and translucent.
Add the shredded chicken and stock. Bring to the boil before turning down the heat and allowing to simmer for 45 minutes.
Add the noodles, marjoram and thyme 5 minutes before the end of cooking. Season to taste.

# SPICY BUTTERNUT SQUASH
## for 8

This soup is rich and spicy and especially popular at Thanksgiving and Hallowe'en. The seeds of the squash can be a delicious garnish: use a spoon to extricate them before cleaning off any bits of flesh and placing on a baking tray. Drizzle with olive oil, sprinkle with salt and freshly ground black pepper and place in the oven at 150°C for 5–8 minutes – be careful as they do have a tendency to pop if they get too hot. Drizzle chilli oil or extra virgin olive oil over each bowl of soup and scatter with seeds. This soup freezes very well.

Ingredients

1 large onion, diced
1 clove garlic, crushed
1 small red chilli, seeds removed and finely sliced
1 lemongrass stalk, hard outer leaves removed and soft core finely chopped
½ teaspoon peeled and grated fresh ginger
2 medium butternut squash, seeds removed, peeled, and cut into chunks
1 tin full fat coconut milk
2 litres vegetable stock (p.98)
1 tablespoon fresh coriander, finely chopped
olive oil
salt and freshly ground black pepper

Method

In a large heavy based saucepan, sweat the onion in a little olive oil on a low heat for about 10 minutes until soft and translucent.
Add the garlic, ginger, lemongrass and chilli. Sweat for a further 2 minutes.
Add the butternut squash and vegetable stock. Bring to the boil before turning down the heat and allowing to simmer for 40 minutes or until the squash is soft.
Remove from the heat and stir in the coconut milk.
Blend with a hand stick blender until smooth.
Season to taste.

# CUCUMBER & MINT
## for 6

A delicious starter during the summer months, this soup is a firm Finns favourite. If you want to have this ready on the table, it is a good idea to chill the serving bowls in the fridge before ladling out the soup and garnishing with diced cucumber, freshly chopped chives and mint leaves. Not suitable for freezing.

Ingredients

4 spring onions, finely chopped
2 cloves garlic, crushed
4 large cucumbers, peeled and roughly chopped
160ml dry white wine
600g full fat natural yoghurt
4 tablespoons whipping cream
2 teaspoons of fresh lemon juice
½ teaspoon runny honey
small handful fresh mint, finely chopped
salt and freshly ground black pepper

Method

Using a hand stick blender, blend together the spring onions, garlic, cucumber, white wine and mint.
Pour into a large bowl and stir in the yoghurt, cream, lemon juice and honey.
Mix well and season to taste.
Place in the fridge for a minimum of 4 hours to chill.

# Asparagus Vichyssoise
for 6

This is Katie's favourite soup. She developed the recipe as a way of using the wonderful fresh asparagus grown so easily in Norfolk. Once the asparagus season is over, Katie uses samphire which she picks on walks along the Norfolk coast or buys from Rex at The Chelsea Fishmonger.

Ingredients

450g asparagus
3 large leeks, green removed
2 medium Maris Piper potatoes, peeled and diced
40g salted butter
700ml vegetable stock (p.98)
100ml double cream
100ml full fat Greek yoghurt
zest of 1 lemon
1 teaspoon caster sugar
small handful fresh parsley, finely chopped
olive oil
extra virgin olive oil
salt and freshly ground black pepper

Method

Snap off the woody ends of the asparagus and discard.
Cut the asparagus into 2cm long pieces and keep the tips separate from the stalks.
Finely slice the leeks and rinse them in a colander to remove any dirt.
In a large heavy based saucepan, melt the butter and sweat the vegetables and lemon zest excluding the asparagus tips for 5 minutes, keeping the heat low so that the vegetables do not colour.
Add the stock and sugar and bring to the boil before lowering the heat. Allow to simmer for 40 minutes.

Remove from the heat and blend with a hand stick blender until smooth.
Use a metal spoon or a plastic spatula to fold in the cream and half of the yoghurt.
Allow to cool before refrigerating.
Bring a pan of salted water to the boil. Add the asparagus tips and cook for 1 minute. Remove and refresh in iced water. Toss in extra virgin olive oil, salt and pepper.
To serve, pour the soup into chilled bowls, add a spoonful of the remaining yoghurt to each, sprinkle with the asparagus tips and the freshly chopped parsley.

# Stocks

*I feel a recipe is only a theme, which an intelligent cook can play each time with a variation.*
MADAME BENOIT

Vegetable Stock
Chicken Stock
Beef Stock

At Finns we make fresh stock in large batches each day. We recommend that you do the same and freeze the excess to be used as and when you need it.

## VEGETABLE STOCK
makes 2 litres

Ingredients

3 litres of water
2 large onions, skin on and quartered
1 bunch of celery including the leaves, roughly chopped
5 medium carrots, roughly chopped
1 bouquet garni of fresh parsley stalks, fresh sprigs of thyme, a bay leaf and fresh tarragon
5 whole black peppercorns

Method

Place all the ingredients into a stock pot.
Bring to the boil before turning down the heat and allowing to simmer for 1 hour, placing a lid on the pot.

Strain the stock into a jug, discarding the vegetables, bouquet garni and peppercorns.
Allow to cool and freeze in quantities of 1 litre.
Defrost the stock in the fridge the night before needed.

# CHICKEN STOCK
makes 3 litres

Ingredients

4 litres of water
2–3 chicken carcasses
1 large onion, skin on and quartered
1 medium carrot, roughly chopped
2 large celery stalks, roughly chopped
1 bouquet garni of fresh parsley stalks, fresh sprigs of thyme, a bay leaf and fresh tarragon
5 whole black peppercorns

Method

Place all the ingredients into a stock pot.
Bring to the boil before turning down the heat and simmering for 1½ hours, placing a lid on the pot. Skim the fat off the surface of the stock 2–3 times during the process.
Strain the stock into a jug, discarding the carcasses, vegetables, bouquet garni and peppercorns.
Allow to cool and freeze in quantities of 1 litre.
Defrost the stock in the fridge the night before needed.

# BEEF STOCK
makes 4 litres

Ingredients

5 litres of water
2.5kg beef bones
handful of beef trimmings
1 large onion, skin on and quartered
4 medium carrots, roughly chopped
1 bouquet garni of fresh parsley stalks, fresh sprigs of thyme, a bay leaf and fresh tarragon
1 tablespoon tomato purée
5 whole black peppercorns

Method

Preheat the oven to 180°C.
Put the bones and trimmings in a roasting tray and roast for 30 minutes.
Add the vegetables and roast for a further 15 minutes. Allow to cool.
Remove the fat from the beef and vegetable roasting tray and place the contents into a stock pot.
Add the bouquet garni, tomato purée, peppercorns and water.
Bring to a boil before turning down the heat and allowing to simmer for 3–4 hours, placing a lid on the saucepan. Skim the fat off the surface of the stock 2–3 times during the process.
Strain the stock into a jug, discarding the bones, trimmings, vegetables, bouquet garni and peppercorns.
Allow to cool and freeze in quantities of 1 litre.
Defrost the stock in the fridge the night before needed.

# Paté

*A customer is our most important visitor. He is not dependent on us, we are dependent on him.*
*He is not an interruption to our work, he is the purpose of it. He is not an outsider in our*
*business, he is part of it. We are not doing him a favour by serving him. He is doing us a favour*
*by giving us the opportunity to do so.*
MOHANDAS GANDHI

Chicken Liver
Smoked Trout
Chunky Salmon and Prawn with Savoury Biscotti

The quantities listed for the patés are for starter portions.

## CHICKEN LIVER PATÉ
for 6

For years, our upstairs neighbour was a man named Mr Wilkinson. He and his wife loved this paté and we would always give him any pots that did not quite make the necessary weight for selling in the shop.

This rich paté is delicious when spread on crispy crostini and topped with Finns red onion marmalade or served with melba toast. It is very popular during the picnic season especially with men going to Lords, Twickenham or Henley. It will last for 1 week in the fridge and freezes successfully.

Ingredients for the paté

500g chicken livers
125g unsalted butter, cubed and cold
1 small onion, diced
1 clove garlic, crushed

1 teaspoon fresh thyme leaves
1 teaspoon brandy
1 teaspoon of fresh lemon juice
½ teaspoon Tabasco
vegetable oil
salt and freshly ground black pepper

Ingredients for the clarified butter

125g unsalted butter

Method to make the paté

Trim all the stringy bits of sinew and fat from the livers.
In a large heavy based frying pan, sweat the onion in a little vegetable oil on a low heat for 10 minutes until soft and translucent.
Add the garlic and thyme and sweat for a further 2 minutes.
Turn up the heat and add the chicken livers. Cook the livers until just past pink.
Add the brandy to the pan and flambé.
Pour the mixture into a food processor. Add the Tabasco and lemon juice and blend. Whilst processing, add the cold cubed butter, cube by cube until the paté is smooth.
Season to taste and pour into 6 ramekins or a pretty bowl.
Chill in the fridge for 2 hours before topping with clarified butter.

Method to make the clarified butter

Melt the butter in a pan until it bubbles.
Allow to cool slightly. With a spoon remove the white bubbles from the top of the melted butter and discard.
Top the paté with a little of the still melted butter being careful not to allow the white impurities at the bottom of the pan to mix with the clarified butter on top. The butter should be about 2mm in thickness on top of the paté.
Place the topped patés in the fridge to set for about 1 hour, or overnight.

# SMOKED TROUT PATÉ
## for 6

This is our most popular paté. Sourcing the best smoked trout you can is extremely important for this simple but moreish recipe. Serve with buttered brown toast and lemon wedges.

Ingredients

4 fillets of smoked trout
1 tablespoon horseradish sauce
200–250g mayonnaise (below)
zest and juice of ½ a lemon
freshly ground black pepper

Method

Place the trout into a food processor and pulse to a coarse consistency.
Transfer to bowl and gently fold in the horseradish sauce, mayonnaise, lemon zest and juice and freshly ground black pepper.
Place into 6 ramekins or a pretty bowl and refrigerate until needed.

# MAYONNAISE
## makes 350ml

When making mayonnaise in the shop, we use pasteurised egg yolks but, at home, I use good free range eggs as in this recipe.

Ingredients

2 egg yolks
¼ teaspoon Dijon mustard
225ml vegetable oil
1 tablespoon white wine vinegar

¼ teaspoon salt
freshly ground black pepper

Method

In a dry bowl, whisk together the egg yolks, mustard, white wine vinegar and salt.
Whisking constantly, add the oil very slowly in a thin stream. Placing the bowl on a damp tea towel ensures the bowl stays still leaving your hands free to whisk the mayonnaise and pour in the oil.
Add salt and freshly ground black pepper to taste.

# CHUNKY SALMON & PRAWN PATÉ WITH SAVOURY BISCOTTI
for 6

I make these biscotti in a large batch as they are always useful for starters or as the basis of a cocktail eat. They keep for 2 months in an airtight container and the recipe below makes 22. The fennel seeds in this recipe make them a great partner for the paté.

Ingredients for the biscotti

250g plain white flour
100g pine nuts
50g parmesan, grated
100g pitted green olives, finely chopped
3 eggs, very lightly beaten
1 teaspoon baking powder
1 teaspoon fennel seeds
pinch of freshly ground black pepper

Method for the biscotti

Preheat the oven to 180°C.
Line a baking tray with greaseproof paper.
Place all the dry ingredients into a large bowl, make a well and add the eggs,
slowly mixing to form a smooth dough. The dough will be quite solid.
Form into a rough log shape, about 22cm by 4cm and bake for 20 minutes.
Remove from the oven and allow to cool.
Reduce the heat of the oven to 80°C.
Using a serrated knife, cut the biscotti into 1cm thick slices.
Place the slices on a baking tray in a single layer.
Return to the oven and allow to dry out for 1 hour.

Ingredients for the paté

150g small prawns, cooked and shelled
150g smoked salmon, cut into thin strips
400g full fat cream cheese
zest and juice of ½ a lemon
1 tablespoon fresh dill, finely chopped
freshly ground black pepper

Method for the paté

Mix the smoked salmon, prawns and cream cheese in a bowl, being careful
not to break up the prawns.
Add the lemon juice, zest and dill and mix well.
Season to taste and garnish with extra fresh dill.

# Quiche and Pastry

*Feeding people graciously and lovingly is one of life's simplest pleasures: a most basic way of making life better for someone, at least for a while.*
ANNA THOMAS

Ham, Courgette and Parmesan Quiche
3 Cheese and Leek Quiche
Savoury Shortcrust Pastry
Sweet Shortcrust Pastry

It is the quality of our eggs which make the following recipes so delicious. During the early years, we sold cracked eggs from a large wicker basket in the shop. We sourced them from an Oxfordshire farm and stocked them until Edwina Curry put her stamp on the egg industry and we fell casualty to the rules and regulations of the food police from The Royal Borough of Kensington and Chelsea who prevented us selling these inexpensive fresh eggs because of the very cracks which made them so cheap.

Each day at Finns, we make several quiches and a slice of freshly baked quiche with two salads is one the most popular dishes available in the café. The fillings are extremely versatile: roasted vegetables, salmon and pea, slow roast red onion and asparagus and gruyère are all delicious. The two recipes below are the most popular at Finns.

# Ham, Courgette & Parmesan Quiche
makes 1 x 30cm tart, enough for 12 generous servings

Ingredients

1 quantity of savoury shortcrust pastry at room temperature (see p.109 in this section)
1 egg, lightly whisked with which to brush the pastry
1 large onion, diced
1 large courgette, grated
200g top quality ham, cut into small chunks
75g mature cheddar cheese, coarsely grated
120g parmesan, grated
3 eggs
enough double cream to make up 800ml when combined with the eggs
salt and freshly ground black pepper

Method

Preheat the oven to 180°c.
Roll out the pastry and line the quiche tin with it. Make sure that the pastry overhangs the edges of the tin by about 1cm as it shrinks whilst it cooks.
Place the pastry into the freezer for 20 minutes.
Remove from the freezer and bake blind for 30 minutes.
Remove the baking beans and brush the pastry with the beaten egg before baking for a further 4 minutes, until golden brown.

In a frying pan, sweat the onion in a little oil on a low heat for about 10 minutes until soft and translucent.
In a large bowl, mix the courgette, ham, cheddar and parmesan with the cooked onion.
Place this mixture in the pastry shell.
In a jug, whisk the eggs, cream, salt and freshly ground black pepper together.
Pour the egg and cream mixture into the pastry case.
Bake for about 30 minutes or until the quiche is just set and golden brown.

# 3 Cheese & Leek Quiche

makes 1 x 30cm tart, enough for 12 generous servings

Ingredients

1 quantity of savoury shortcrust pastry at room temperature (see p. 109 in this section)
1 egg, lightly whisked with which to brush the pastry
1 knob of unsalted butter
2 leeks, finely sliced
100g crumbled goat's cheese
100g parmesan, grated
75g mature cheddar cheese, grated
3 eggs
enough double cream to make up 800ml when combined with the eggs
salt and freshly ground black pepper

Method

Preheat the oven to 180°C.
Roll out the pastry and line the quiche tin with it. Make sure that the pastry overhangs the edges of the tin by about 1cm as it shrinks whilst it cooks.
Place the pastry into the freezer for 20 minutes.
Remove from the freezer and bake blind for 30 minutes.
Remove the baking beans and brush the pastry with the beaten egg before baking for a further 4 minutes, until golden brown.

In a frying pan, melt a knob of butter and sweat the leeks on a low heat for about 10 minutes until soft, seasoning with salt and pepper.
In a large bowl, mix the 3 cheeses and cooked leeks.
Place the leek and cheese mixture into the pastry shell.
In a jug, whisk the eggs, cream, salt and freshly ground black pepper together.
Pour the egg and cream mixture into the pastry case.
Bake for about 30 minutes or until the quiche is just set and golden brown.

# Savoury Shortcrust Pastry
makes 1 x 30cm tart, enough for 12 generous servings

To make the best pastry, try to keep your hands cool and work quickly, handling the pastry for as short a time as possible. It is a very useful thing to have in the freezer. The 2 pastries listed below can be used for numerous recipes.

Ingredients

110g plain white flour
25g lard, cold and cubed
25g unsalted butter, cold and cubed
2 tablespoons water
pinch of salt

Method

Rub the butter and flour together until the mixture resembles the consistency of breadcrumbs.
Add the water, one tablespoon at a time until the pastry loosely binds together.
Form the pastry into a ball and wrap it in cling film.
Place in the fridge and leave it to rest for a minimum of 1 hour. The pastry is now ready to be used or frozen.

# Sweet Shortcrust Pastry
makes 1 x 30cm tart, enough for 12 generous servings

Ingredients

220g plain white flour
100g unsalted butter, cold
100g caster sugar
2 egg yolks, beaten
2 teaspoons vanilla essence

Method

Rub the butter and flour together until the mixture resembles the consistency of breadcrumbs.
Gradually add the egg yolks and vanilla essence until the pastry loosely binds together.
Form the pastry into a ball and wrap it in cling film.
Place in the fridge and leave it to rest for a minimum of 1 hour. The pastry is now ready to be used or frozen.

# Starters

*To invite a person into your house is to take charge of his happiness*
*for as long as he is under your roof.*
A Brillat-Savarin

Spinach Roulade with Smoked Salmon and Cream Cheese
Celeriac Remoulade with Crispy Prosciutto and Apple
Lemon and Dill Celeriac with Tiger Prawns
Marinated and Seared Tuna with Courgette Ribbons and Pink Peppercorns
Pea Falafel with Rocket and Pea Shoots
Figs with Robiola and Parma Ham
Beef Carpaccio

## Spinach Roulade
## with Smoked Salmon & Cream Cheese
### makes 1 roulade, enough for 8 thick slices

Marina's favourite recipe, this retro roulade is a lovely starter or light lunch. It has been popular at Finns for twenty-seven years. Serve one slice on the centre of each plate surrounded by rocket or mixed leaves dressed with extra virgin olive oil and lemon. Alternatively slice thinly and place on a plate of smoked salmon. If you wish to make this recipe suitable for vegetarians, replace the smoked salmon with sun-blushed tomatoes.

Ingredients

1 kg raw spinach, stalks removed
3 eggs

150g full fat crème fraîche
100g parmesan, grated
60g self-raising white flour
4 tablespoons full fat cream cheese
8 slices smoked salmon
juice of ½ a lemon
vegetable oil, for greasing
salt and freshly ground black pepper

Method

Preheat the oven to 180°c.
Line a 28cm x 38cm Swiss roll tin with greaseproof paper brushed with a little vegetable oil.
Place well washed spinach in a large saucepan and heat gently until wilted. Remove and allow to cool.
Place the spinach in a colander, sprinkle with salt and squeeze out all the water.
Separate the eggs placing the whites in a large clean bowl and the egg yolks into a jug.
Whisk the egg yolks together before placing them in a food processor along with the cooked cooled spinach, crème fraîche, flour, parmesan, salt and freshly ground black pepper. Blend until well combined and place in a large bowl.
Whisk the egg whites until they form stiff peaks. Add a large tablespoon of the egg white to the spinach mixture and fold in gently with a plastic spatula or metal spoon. Gently fold in the remaining egg white to the mixture.
Pour the roulade mixture into the Swiss roll tin and bake for 12−15 minutes or until springy to the touch.
Remove from the oven and turn the roulade out onto a clean damp tea towel, peeling off the greaseproof paper. Whilst still warm, roll the roulade with the tea towel, starting at the longest side. Allow to cool.
Unroll the roulade and spread with a layer of cream cheese. Lay the smoked salmon over the cheese. Season with pepper and a squeeze of lemon juice. Using the tea towel to help you, roll the roulade and slice.

# CELERIAC REMOULADE
## WITH CRISPY PROSCIUTTO & APPLE
### for 6

This is a staple dish in all French delicatessens and provincial butchers. The combination of prosciutto and apple with celeriac is one of our most successful starters. It can be made well in advance of eating and is a great picnic stalwart, going well with Finns honey baked ham.

Ingredients

12 slices prosciutto
2 tart green eating apples
1 celeriac, peeled and cut into chunks
250ml mayonnaise (p.103)
zest and juice of 1 lemon
1 tablespoon grainy mustard
1 tablespoon red wine vinegar
1 tablespoon whole milk
handful of fresh chervil and parsley, finely chopped plus extra parsley to garnish
extra virgin olive oil
salt and freshly ground black pepper

Method

Use a cheese grater or a food processor to grate the celeriac. Place in a serving bowl.
In a jug, whisk the mayonnaise, lemon zest, mustard, red wine vinegar and milk together.
Pour the dressing over the celeriac and mix well.
Grate the apples and dress with the lemon juice to stop them browning.
Add the grated apple and chopped herbs to the celeriac. Mix well.
Season to taste and keep refrigerated until needed.

Preheat the oven to 180°C.

Line a baking tray with greaseproof paper. Place the prosciutto onto the baking tray and bake for 5 minutes until crispy.

To serve, make a pile of remoulade in the centre of each serving plate and lay the prosciutto on top. Drizzle with a little extra virgin olive oil and sprinkle with finely chopped fresh parsley.

# LEMON & DILL CELERIAC
# WITH TIGER PRAWNS
for 6

The prawns are a popular alternative to the prosciutto of the previous recipe.

Ingredients

225g large peeled king prawns, cooked
2 slices of preserved lemon, washed very well and cut into very small cubes
zest and juice of 1 lime
1 teaspoon pink peppercorns, lightly crushed in a pestle and mortar
1 tablespoon fresh parsley, finely chopped
1 tablespoon fresh chives, finely chopped
large handful fresh dill, finely chopped
1 celeriac, peeled and cut into large chunks
250ml mayonnaise (p.103)
zest and juice of 1 lemon
1 tablespoon whole milk
3 tablespoons extra virgin olive oil
salt and freshly ground black pepper

Method

Place the prawns, preserved lemon, zest and juice of the lime, peppercorns, parsley, chives and half the dill into a bowl. Coat with 3 tablespoons of extra virgin olive oil and mix well. Leave to marinate for at least 2 hours.

Use a cheese grater or a food processor to grate the celeriac. Place in a serving bowl.

In a jug, whisk the mayonnaise, lemon juice and zest, and milk together.

Pour the dressing over the remoulade, add the remaining dill and mix well. Season to taste.

Pile the remoulade onto 6 serving plates and divide the prawns between each plate, drizzling over a little of the marinade. Serve with watercress and lemon wedges.

# MARINATED & SEARED TUNA WITH COURGETTE RIBBONS & PINK PEPPERCORNS
for 6

Pink peppercorns are not really peppercorns at all but rather a spice made from the dried berries of the Peruvian peppercorn tree. Lightly peppery, their pink hue gives this dish a wonderful vibrancy. It is important to buy the best tuna available. We ask our fishmonger for sashimi grade tuna; the texture and flavour is extraordinary and well worth the extra cost.

Ingredients

600g tuna steak
3 large courgettes
zest of 1 lemon
zest of 1 lime
large handful mixed fresh herbs, finely chopped: dill, coriander, parsley
24 pink peppercorns, lightly crushed in a pestle and mortar
olive oil
4 tablespoons extra virgin olive oil
salt and freshly ground black pepper

Method the night before

Place the tuna steak into a bowl and cover with the lemon and lime zest, herbs, peppercorns, a little black pepper and extra virgin olive oil. Do not add any salt or lemon/lime juice at this stage as it will toughen and discolour the tuna.
Cover the bowl with cling film and leave to marinate in the fridge overnight.

Method on the day

Remove the tuna from the fridge and allow to reach room temperature.
Use a potato peeler to peel the courgettes into long thin ribbons.
Drizzle the slices with a little olive oil and season lightly with salt and freshly ground black pepper.
Heat a griddle pan until smoking hot.
Griddle the courgettes for about 3 seconds on each side until you can see the griddle lines and set aside.
Remove the tuna from the marinade, reserving the marinade for later use.
Use the hot griddle pan to sear the tuna steak. It will take about 30 seconds for each side.
Once seared, slice the tuna into thin slices.
Lay the courgette ribbons in the centre of a large platter and place the slices of tuna around the edge. Drizzle with the remaining marinade.

## PEA FALAFEL WITH ROCKET & PEA SHOOTS
makes 24 small falafel – serves 6

The falafel make a wonderful starter loosely assembled with the salad leaves. Adding roasted butternut squash turns the starter into an excellent vegetarian main course. Any left over falafel can be popped into wraps or pitta bread with hummus for hasty mid-week lunches. The falafel can be cooked in advance and combined with the salad leaves at the last minute. Serve with a dollop of sour cream on the side of each plate.

Ingredients

250g peas
2 medium shallots, diced
1 small red chilli, seeds removed and finely chopped
1 egg
50g fresh white breadcrumbs
1 teaspoon ground cumin
1 teaspoon sesame seeds
small handful fresh coriander, finely chopped
2 large handfuls of rocket leaves
2 large handfuls of mixed bean shoots
salt and freshly ground black pepper
2 tablespoons vegetable oil
extra virgin olive oil
zest of 1 lemon, to garnish
small pot of sour cream

Method

Bring a pan of salted water to the boil. Add the peas and boil for 2 minutes.
Drain and refresh in iced water.
In a frying pan, sweat the shallots in a little olive oil on a low heat for about
3 minutes until soft and translucent.
Add the ground cumin, sesame seeds and chilli and cook for a further 3
minutes.
Place the cooked shallot mixture into a food processor with the peas. Blend
for 5 seconds until coarsely ground.
Add the coriander and the egg to the food processor and blend until well
combined. Place in a bowl, mix in the breadcrumbs and season.
Lightly flour your hands and form the falafel mixture into 24 even balls.
Gently flatten the balls into thick discs.
Heat the vegetable oil in a deep frying pan and fry the falafel on each side
until golden brown.
Allow the hot falafel to cool slightly before combining with the pea shoots
and rocket. Drizzle with a little extra virgin olive oil and grated lemon zest.

# FIGS WITH ROBIOLA & PARMA HAM
## for 6

This is a lovely summer salad and works equally well with peaches or nectarines or a combination of them both. Aged balsamic vinegar is thicker than young balsamic and makes this dressing sweet and sticky. Robiola is a soft-ripened Italian cheese which is worth seeking out.

Ingredients

6 ripe figs
6 slices Parma ham
150g robiola cheese
4 large handfuls of a mixture of lamb's leaf lettuce and watercress
aged balsamic vinegar
juice of ½ a lemon
extra virgin olive oil
salt and freshly ground black pepper

Method

Trim the stalks of the figs and almost cut each fig into quarters, nearly cutting down to the bottom of the fruit. Gently open the fruit out, pinching at the base so that the inside flesh is displayed. Place a small spoonful of robiola in each fig.
Dress the salad leaves with a little olive oil, lemon, salt and freshly ground black pepper.
Lay a slice of Parma ham loosely on each plate, with a small heap of salad. Place a fig on the side and drizzle with the balsamic vinegar before serving.

# BEEF CARPACCIO
## for 6

This is a variation on the classic beef carpaccio. It looks lovely when served from a large platter garnished with a few rocket leaves and some extra virgin olive oil. With relatively few ingredients, it is important that each component is of the best quality available, especially the beef.

Ingredients

600g beef fillet
100g rocket leaves
75g ricotta
70g shaved parmesan
small handful pine nuts, toasted
zest of 1 lemon
olive oil
extra virgin olive oil
salt and freshly ground black pepper

Method

Trim and clean the fillet, removing all the sinew and fat.
Rub with olive oil and season with salt and freshly ground black pepper.
Heat a griddle pan until smoking hot. Sear the meat on all sides.
Remove from the heat and allow the beef to rest for 5–10 minutes in the fridge.
Meanwhile, mix the ricotta, 50g of the parmesan and half the pine nuts together in a bowl with the lemon zest and some freshly ground black pepper.
Remove the beef from the fridge and slice it as thinly as you can with the sharpest knife you own.
Place each piece of sliced beef between two pieces of cling film and use a rolling pin to roll and flatten them until almost translucent. Cut each piece in half.
Spread with a fine layer of the ricotta mixture. Top with a layer of rocket leaves and roll into a cigar shape.
Divide the cigars between each plate, season with freshly ground rock salt, the remaining parmesan and a scattering of the remaining pine nuts.
Lightly drizzle with extra virgin olive oil.

# Fish

In the 16th and 17th centuries, many Chelsea residents made their living from fishing. In 1598, John Stow conducted a survey of London in which he stated that there was no river in Europe to compare with the Thames in its London reaches for "fat, sweet salmon being taken daily from the stream."

Salmon with Basil Pesto
Salmon with Broad Beans, Chilli and Dill
Salmon with Ginger and Almonds
Salmon Fish Cakes with Cucumber and Tomato Salsa
Luxury Fish Pie
Cod with Chorizo, Cherry Tomatoes and Olives
Cod with Prawns and Dill
Creamy Mustard Cod
Prawn and Ginger Egg Fried Rice

## SALMON WITH BASIL PESTO
for 6

We use organic Scottish salmon in all our recipes – the farmed variety being so inferior in taste and texture.

The pesto for this dish can be made in advance. We like to make triple the quantity listed below and store it in a jar in the fridge. Every time we use some, we cover the remainder with a little more extra virgin olive oil so that it stays fresh. This pesto will last for 2 weeks in the fridge. In the absence of good fresh basil, handfuls of rocket or watercress can be substituted. When

Milly visits her in-laws in Cumbria in spring, she returns with wild garlic from Levens and the leaves of this pungent plant give the pesto a wonderful depth of flavour when substituted for the basil.

Ingredients

6 skinless salmon fillets, weighing 150g–200g each
zest of 1 lemon
extra virgin olive oil
salt and freshly ground black pepper

Ingredients for the pesto, makes about 400ml

115g fresh basil leaves
30g pine nuts
50g parmesan, grated
1 clove garlic, peeled
squeeze of lemon juice
150ml extra virgin olive oil

Method to make the pesto

In a food processor, blend the pine nuts, parmesan, garlic and half the olive oil for 30 seconds.
Add the basil and slowly pour in the remaining oil as the mixture processes.

Method to cook the salmon

Preheat the grill to a high heat.
Lay the salmon on a baking sheet or a grill tray. Season the fish with salt, freshly ground black pepper and the lemon zest.
Drizzle with extra virgin olive oil and grill for 7 minutes.
Place a tablespoon of pesto on each salmon fillet and serve.

# SALMON WITH BROAD BEANS, CHILLI & DILL
## for 6

Frozen or fresh broad beans can be used in the recipe. If possible, freeze large batches of fresh broad beans when they are in season (June to September). This dish can be served hot or cold.

Ingredients

6 skinless salmon fillets, weighing 150g–200g each
400g broad beans
1 small red chilli, seeds removed and finely sliced
zest of 2 lemons
small handful fresh dill, finely chopped
extra virgin olive oil
salt and freshly ground black pepper

Method

Bring a pan of salted water to the boil.
Add the broad beans and boil for 3 minutes.
Drain and refresh in iced water.
Peel off the outer, greeny-grey skin from the broad bean and place the beans in a bowl. Add the chilli, zest of 1 lemon, dill and extra virgin olive oil and mix well.
Preheat the grill to a high heat.
Lay the salmon on a baking sheet or a grill tray. Season the fish with salt, freshly ground black pepper and the zest of 1 lemon.
Drizzle with extra virgin olive oil and grill for 7 minutes.
Scatter the broad beans, chilli and dill over the salmon to serve.

# SALMON WITH GINGER & ALMONDS
## for 6

The simplicity of this dish makes it perfect for a mid-week supper. Serve with brown rice, lightly steamed broccoli or pak choi.

Ingredients

6 skinless salmon fillets, weighing 150g–200g each
zest of 1 lemon
6 teaspoons stem ginger paste (see Notes on p.88)
100g flaked almonds
extra virgin olive oil
salt and freshly ground black pepper

Method

Preheat the oven to 180°C.
Place the almonds on a baking tray and bake for 5 minutes until lightly toasted.
Preheat the grill to a high heat.
Lay the salmon on a baking sheet or a grill tray. Spread a teaspoon of the stem ginger paste on each fillet. Season the fish with salt, freshly ground black pepper and lemon zest.
Drizzle with extra virgin olive oil and grill for 7 minutes.
Place on serving plates and scatter with the toasted flaked almonds.

# SALMON FISH CAKES
# WITH CUCUMBER & TOMATO SALSA
makes 12 cakes

Serve these fish cakes with home made potato wedges, as a variation on fish and chips. Alternatively, serve as a light lunch with lemon wedges, aïoli (p. 140) and the salsa.

Ingredients for the fish cakes

400g skinless salmon fillets
800g baking potatoes, peeled and cut into quarters
1 medium onion, diced
zest and juice of 1 lemon, plus 2 slices to flavour the fish poaching liquid
1 heaped teaspoon horseradish sauce
1 heaped dessertspoon mayonnaise (p. 103)
5 whole black peppercorns
small handful fresh parsley, finely chopped
small handful fresh dill, finely chopped
3 eggs, beaten
100g plain white flour, seasoned with a little salt and freshly ground black pepper
100g fresh white breadcrumbs
200ml vegetable oil

Ingredients for the salsa

half a large cucumber, seeds removed
4 large sweet tomatoes, seeds removed
1 medium red chilli, seeds removed and finely sliced
zest and juice of 1 lime
small handful fresh parsley, finely chopped
salt and freshly ground black pepper

Method for the salsa

Finely dice the cucumber and tomatoes.
Place the diced vegetables into a sieve and place over a bowl. Sprinkle with salt and allow the excess water to drip away (about 15 minutes).
Mix the diced vegetables with the chilli, lime juice and zest, parsley, salt and freshly ground black pepper.
Keep refrigerated until needed.

Method for the fish cakes

Place the potatoes in a large saucepan, cover in cold water and add a large pinch of salt.
Bring to the boil and cook until very tender. Drain well and place the potatoes in a large baking tray to dry. Once cooled, crush into small chunks with your hands.
Place the salmon in a saucepan and cover with cold water.
Add the peppercorns and lemon slices and bring to a gentle simmer for 8 minutes.
Remove the salmon and flake into a large bowl.
In a food processor, blend the onion, horseradish sauce, mayonnaise, lemon zest and juice, parsley and dill.
Add this mixture and the potatoes to the flaked fish. Mix well and season.
Form the fish cakes into evenly sized patties. This mixture should make 12–14.
Put the flour, eggs and breadcrumbs into separate bowls. Coat each fish cake in flour, then egg, then breadcrumbs.
Place 200ml vegetable oil in a pan and heat over a low heat.
Shallow fry the fish cakes until golden brown.
Serve with the salsa.

# LUXURY FISH PIE
## for 6

This rich, creamy and comforting pie is good for parties large and small. Always a Friday favourite, this is the luxury fish pie that we make for orders in the shop but the shellfish can be removed and replaced with extra haddock and salmon.

Ingredients for the fish pie filling

200g skinless un-dyed smoked haddock
350g skinless salmon fillets
12 king prawns, cooked and shelled
12 scallops
2 medium leeks, finely sliced
800ml whole milk
zest and juice of 1 lemon
1 bay leaf

Ingredients for the white sauce

60g plain white flour
60g unsalted butter
1 tablespoon Dijon mustard

Ingredients for the mash

1kg Desirée or King Edward potatoes
250ml whole milk
50g unsalted butter
50g mature cheddar cheese, grated
salt and freshly ground black pepper

Method to cook the fish

Preheat the oven to 190°C.

Place the milk, peppercorns and bay leaf in a large saucepan and bring to simmering point.
Add the haddock and the salmon and simmer for 10 minutes. Remove and allow to cool, reserving the poaching liquid for the white sauce.
Heat a little olive oil in a frying pan and sear the scallops for about 30 seconds on each side. Set aside.
Break up the haddock and salmon and transfer to a bowl. Scatter the zest and squeeze the juice of the lemon over the fish. Place the shellfish in a separate bowl.

In a large frying pan, melt a large knob of butter and sweat the leeks on a low heat for about 10 minutes until soft, seasoning with salt and pepper. Add the leeks to the haddock and salmon.

Method to make the white sauce

In a pan, melt the butter.
Remove from the heat and incorporate the flour into the butter.
Return to the heat and cook the flour and butter mixture for 2 minutes, whisking well.
Slowly add the reserved poaching milk, whisking constantly to make a thick white sauce. Once the sauce begins to bubble, it is ready.
Mix in the Dijon mustard and season with salt and freshly ground black pepper.

Pour the white sauce into the bowl with the haddock, salmon and leeks and gently mix together so as not to break up the fish. Pour the fish mix into an oven proof dish and top with the prawns and scallops.
Allow to cool.

Method to make the mashed potatoes

Place the potatoes in a large saucepan, cover in cold water and add a large pinch of salt.
Bring to the boil and cook until very tender. Drain.
In a small saucepan, heat the milk and butter until barely simmering.
Mash the potatoes and add the heated milk and butter.
Season well.
Top the fish pie with the potato and cover with the grated cheese.
Place in the oven for 30–40 minutes or until the top is golden brown and the pie is bubbling.

# COD WITH CHORIZO, CHERRY TOMATOES & OLIVES
## for 6

This colourful dish works well with brown rice and pan-fried courgettes. The mild flavour of the fish contrasts with the punchy chorizo and salty olives. It is a simple dish to prepare and looks impressive at a dinner party. When choosing the chorizo, look for one with a high paprika content – Brindisa is a great choice. This gives the dish its fantastic colour and smoky taste.

Ingredients

6 skinless cod fillets, weighing 150g–200g each
500g chorizo, cut into 1cm slices
18 cherry tomatoes, halved
150g black and green pitted Kalamata olives
2 large handfuls baby spinach
1 clove garlic, crushed
extra virgin olive oil
salt and freshly ground black pepper

Method

In a frying pan, fry the chorizo for 3 minutes until crispy. Do not add any oil to the pan as the fat from the chorizo will be sufficient.

Remove the chorizo with a slotted spoon and place on kitchen towel. Add the tomatoes and garlic to the same pan and fry for 8–10 minutes on a low heat, until the tomatoes 'pop.'

Meanwhile, preheat the grill to a high heat.

Lay the cod on a baking sheet or a grill tray. Season the fish with salt and freshly ground black pepper. Drizzle with extra virgin olive oil and grill for 8–10 minutes.

Add the olives to the tomatoes and garlic and fry for a further 2 minutes. Return the chorizo to the pan and cook until piping hot.

Remove from the heat and mix in the spinach, allowing it to wilt from the residual heat of the pan.

Place the cod on warmed plates and spoon over the tomato, olive, chorizo and spinach mixture.

## COD WITH PRAWNS & DILL
### for 6

This dish is beautiful to look at with its delicate whites, pinks and greens. One of our favourite customers regularly orders this as a light Friday night supper before embarking on a summer fishing weekend with friends.

Ingredients

6 skinless cod fillets, weighing 150g–200g each
400g king prawns, raw and shelled
500ml single cream
200ml white wine
1 medium onion, diced
zest and juice of 1 lemon
handful fresh dill, finely chopped

olive oil
extra virgin olive oil
salt and freshly ground black pepper

Method

In a heavy based frying pan, sweat the onion in a little olive oil on a low heat for about 10 minutes until soft and translucent.
Add the lemon juice and zest and half the dill, cooking for a further 2 minutes.
Add the white wine and cream. Bring to the boil before turning down the heat and allowing the sauce to reduce for 3–5 minutes.
Season with salt and freshly ground black pepper and add the prawns.
Cook for 2 minutes, until the prawns are pink and cooked through.
Preheat the grill to a high heat.
Lay the cod on a baking sheet or a grill tray. Season the fish with salt and freshly ground black pepper. Drizzle with extra virgin olive oil and grill for 8–10 minutes.
Make sure the sauce is warm before pouring over the cod to serve, sprinkling each fillet with the remaining dill.

# CREAMY MUSTARD COD
for 6

A firm favourite with many of our customers, this dish has been in the Finns repertoire for twenty-seven years.

Ingredients

6 skinless cod fillets, each weighing 150g–200g each
500ml double cream
1 tablespoon grainy mustard
1 teaspoon Dijon mustard

100ml vegetable stock (p.98)
extra virgin olive oil
salt and freshly ground black pepper

Method

Preheat the grill to a high heat.
Lay the cod on a baking sheet or a grill tray. Season the fish with salt and freshly ground black pepper. Drizzle with extra virgin olive oil and grill for 8–10 minutes.
Place the cream, mustards and stock in a saucepan.
Reduce the sauce by half making sure the cream does not boil.
Season and pour over the cod to serve.

# PRAWN & GINGER EGG FRIED RICE
### for 6 to 8

One of our most popular hot lunches, this dish is perfect for hungry teenagers and great for an informal gathering with only a fork needed. This stir fry should be served with soy and sweet chilli sauce on the side. A mixture of sugar snap peas and bean sprouts can be used to replace the prawns if looking to create a vegetarian main course.

Ingredients

500g king prawns, cooked and shelled
450g basmati rice
2 eggs, lightly beaten
1 lemongrass stalk, outer hard leaves removed and soft centre cut into 1cm pieces
1 medium onion, finely sliced
1 clove garlic, crushed
1 small red chilli, seeds removed and finely sliced

1 teaspoon peeled and grated fresh ginger
250ml sweet chilli sauce
1 tablespoon sesame oil
1 tablespoon fish sauce
1 tablespoon rice vinegar
zest and juice of 1 lime
4 spring onions, finely chopped
vegetable oil
large handful fresh coriander, finely chopped

Method

In a jug, whisk the sweet chilli sauce, sesame oil, fish sauce, rice vinegar, lime juice and zest together.
Wash the rice thoroughly in cold water, place in a large saucepan with the lemongrass and cover in cold water. Add a pinch of salt and bring to the boil, before turning down the heat and cooking until just tender. Drain. Do not overcook the rice as it will continue cooking when added to the wok.
Add a tablespoon of vegetable oil to a wok and place on a high heat.
Once the oil is hot add the onion, garlic, chilli and ginger, stirring constantly.
Add the prawns and mix well with the onion and spices, making sure each prawn is coated in the mixture.
Add the rice and fry until piping hot.
Pour over the eggs and continue frying until the egg is completely cooked (about 1 minute).
Remove from the heat and pour the dressing made earlier over the stir fry.
Pile onto plates and serve immediately, garnishing with the spring onions and fresh coriander.

# Poultry

*It is more important to make classic dishes properly (which means deliciously, with the best available ingredients, following fundamental principles) than just to keep trying to come up with new concoctions just for the sake of originality.*
JULIA CHILD

Coronation Chicken
Pesto Yoghurt Chicken
Chicken Fillets in Lemon and Tarragon
Pea and Herb Chicken
Chicken with Prunes and Leeks
Breaded Chicken Escalopes with Aïoli
Sweet Moroccan Chicken Casserole with Dates, Almonds and Raisins
Thai Green Chicken Curry
Coq au Vin
Poussin Stuffed with Courgettes, Apricots and Pine Nuts
Guinea Fowl with Prosciutto and Madeira
Pheasant in Calvados Cream with Roasted Apples

## CORONATION CHICKEN
for 6

Easily our most popular chicken dish during the summer months, this much beloved recipe graces buffets, lunches and picnic baskets from Glyndebourne to Ascot. During the Queen's Diamond Jubilee in June, we sold more chicken coronation than Milly's and Marisa's body weight combined! Do not be alarmed by the sticky, dark consistency of the marinade – it will alter when mixed with the mayonnaise and crème fraîche.

Ingredients

6 chicken breasts, diced large
2 litres chicken stock (p.99)
1 small onion, diced
1 tablespoon turmeric
3 teaspoons mild curry powder
½ teaspoon ground coriander
½ teaspoon ground nutmeg
½ teaspoon ground cinnamon
½ teaspoon cayenne pepper
½ teaspoon paprika
2 tablespoons best apricot jam
125g mango chutney
250ml mayonnaise (p.103)
250g full fat crème fraîche
vegetable oil

Method

Place the diced chicken in a large saucepan and cover in chicken stock.
Bring to the boil before reducing the heat and simmering for 10–15 minutes
until the chicken is cooked through. Drain and allow to cool.
In a frying pan, sauté the onion in a little vegetable oil.
Add the spices and cook with a further tablespoon of vegetable oil until
fragrant – about five minutes.
Add the apricot jam and mango chutney and cook over a low heat until
melted. Remove to a large bowl and cool.
When cold add the crème fraîche and mayonnaise to the spiced mixture.
Season and add the chicken to the sauce.

# Pesto Yoghurt Chicken

Perfect for buffets and picnics, pesto chicken is another perennial favourite. Cool and creamy, pesto yoghurt sauce makes a change from coronation chicken. You can substitute half the chicken with smoked chicken as an option.

Ingredients for the pesto, makes about 400ml

115g fresh basil leaves
30g pine nuts plus a small handful to garnish
50g parmesan, grated
1 clove garlic, peeled
squeeze of lemon juice
150ml extra virgin olive oil

Ingredients for the chicken

6 chicken breasts, diced large
2 litres chicken stock (p.99)
pesto (above)
150ml mayonnaise (p.103)
500ml full fat natural yoghurt
salt and freshly ground black pepper

Method

In a food processor, blend the pine nuts, parmesan, garlic, lemon juice and half the olive oil for 30 seconds.
Add the basil and blend, slowly adding the remaining oil as the mixture processes.
Place the diced chicken in a large saucepan and cover in chicken stock. Bring to the boil before reducing the heat and simmering for 10–15 minutes until the chicken is cooked through. Drain and allow to cool.
Mix the pesto with the mayonnaise and yoghurt and stir the cooled chicken into the mixture.
Season with salt and freshly ground black pepper to taste.
Garnish with fresh basil and extra pine nuts.

# CHICKEN FILLETS IN LEMON & TARRAGON
for 6

This dish is delicious hot or cold. Serve cold with jewelled couscous (p.177) or hot with buttery tagliatelle. This dish benefits from marinating in the sauce after cooking so it is best to make it in advance and then reheat.

Ingredients

6 chicken breasts, cut in half horizontally
400ml chicken stock (p.99)
200ml extra virgin olive oil
zest and juice of 2 lemons
1 tablespoon Dijon mustard
handful fresh tarragon, finely chopped
salt and freshly ground black pepper

Method

Place the halved chicken breasts between 2 pieces of greaseproof paper and bash with a rolling pin until flattened and even.
Heat a griddle pan until smoking hot and griddle the chicken fillets for 2–3 minutes on each side until cooked through. Set aside in an oven proof dish.
Heat the chicken stock in a saucepan to just below boiling point.
Use a hand stick blender to blend the hot chicken stock, lemon juice and zest, mustard and tarragon. Slowly add the olive oil to the stock in a thin stream, continuing to blend until the sauce ingredients are well combined and emulsified.
Pour the sauce over the chicken and leave for a minimum of 4 hours in the fridge so that the flavours infuse. It is then ready to serve cold. To serve hot, cover and reheat for 20 minutes at 180°C.

# Pea & Herb Chicken
## for 6

This pretty vibrant green chicken dish has become a popular summer favourite and is delicious served cold or hot. This recipe tastes even better if cooked a few hours before you want to eat it as the flavour of the fresh peas and herbs in the sauce work as an excellent marinade for the cooked chicken. It is vital that the peas are not overcooked as it will not only effect the taste, but also the colour of the dish.

Ingredients

6 chicken supremes, skin on
300g frozen peas
200ml white wine
400ml chicken stock (p.99)
200ml extra virgin olive oil
zest and juice of 1 lemon
large handful mixed fresh herbs, finely chopped: parsley, basil and tarragon
2 punnets of pea shoots
salt and freshly ground black pepper

Method

Preheat the oven to 180°C.
Line a baking tray with greaseproof paper.
Heat a griddle pan until smoking hot and griddle the chicken for 2 minutes on the skin side so that it crisps up.
Place on the baking tray and pour the wine and stock over the chicken.
Bake for 25–30 minutes or until the chicken is cooked through.
Remove from the oven and transfer the chicken to an ovenproof dish.
Pour the cooking juices into a saucepan and bring to the boil.
Add 2/3 of the peas and boil for 2 minutes.
Remove from the heat and add the herbs, lemon juice and zest.
Using a hand stick blender, blend the sauce.
Slowly add the olive oil in a thin stream, continuing to blend until the sauce

ingredients are well combined and emulsified. Season to taste.

Pour the sauce over the chicken and leave for a minimum of 4 hours so that the flavours infuse. It is then ready to serve cold. To serve hot, cover and reheat for 25–30 minutes at 180°C. When you are ready to serve, cook the remaining peas, toss in olive oil and use as a garnish with the pea shoots.

# CHICKEN WITH PRUNES & LEEKS
## for 6

One of my favourite recipes, use the fattest, juiciest prunes you can find to make the sauce rich and sweet. I first tasted a similar dish in Normandy and this variation has been a firm Finns favourite ever since. This dish can be made in its entirety in advance. To serve hot, cover and reheat at 180°C for 25–30 minutes.

Ingredients

6 chicken supremes, skin on
200ml white wine
400ml chicken stock (p.99)
200g prunes, pitted and cut in half
3 medium leeks, finely sliced
1 tablespoon fresh thyme leaves
salt and freshly ground black pepper

Method

Preheat the oven to 180°C.
In a large heavy based saucepan, heat a knob of butter and sweat the leeks on a low heat for 10 minutes until soft, seasoning with salt and pepper.
Heat a griddle pan until smoking hot and griddle the chicken for 2 minutes on the skin side so that it crisps up.
Place into a baking tray and pour the wine, stock, cooked leeks and prunes over the chicken. Cover in tin foil and bake for 20 minutes or until cooked through.

Put the chicken into a warmed serving dish. Strain and reserve the cooking juices, placing the prunes and leeks on top of the chicken supremes.

Pour the reserved cooking juices into a saucepan, bring to the boil and reduce by half.

Season before pouring the sauce over the chicken. Serve immediately or allow to cool, to be reheated later.

# Breaded Chicken Escalopes with Aïoli
## for 6

A great dish for children or hungry teenagers, these escalopes can be prepared a day in advance, stored in the fridge and shallow fried just before needed. Alternatively, serve cold, sliced on the diagonal with guacamole for those that run shy of aïoli.

Ingredients

6 chicken breasts, cut in half horizontally
3 eggs, beaten
100g plain white flour, seasoned with a little salt and pepper
100g fresh white breadcrumbs
200ml vegetable oil

Method

Preheat the oven to 180°C.
Place the halved chicken breasts between 2 pieces of greaseproof paper and bash with a rolling pin until flattened and even.
Put the flour, eggs and breadcrumbs into separate bowls. Coat each piece of chicken in flour, then egg, then breadcrumbs.
Place 200ml vegetable oil in a pan and heat over a medium heat.
Shallow fry the chicken until golden brown.
Place in a baking tray and put in the oven for 8–10 minutes.
Serve with aïoli (below).

# Aïoli
makes 350ml

Ingredients

2 egg yolks
¼ teaspoon Dijon mustard
1 clove garlic, crushed
225ml vegetable oil
¼ teaspoon salt
freshly ground black pepper

Method

In a small bowl, whisk together the egg yolks, garlic and mustard.
Whisking constantly, slowly add the oil in a steady stream. Placing the bowl on a damp tea towel ensures the bowl stays still leaving your hands free to whisk whilst pouring in the oil.
Season with salt and freshly ground black pepper.

# Sweet Moroccan Chicken Casserole with Dates, Almonds & Raisins
for 6

This sweet, lightly spiced casserole is delicious served with jewelled couscous (p. 177). This dish works well as bowl food for an informal gathering or buffet.

It is impossible to make small quantities of the Moroccan marinade without compromising the recipe. Make the marinade recipe below but only use the amount quoted in the ingredients for the casserole. Reserve the remainder for another day. It will keep in the fridge for 2 weeks. It is also used in the marinated chickpea with yoghurt and aubergines recipe on page 173 and works well as a marinade for monkfish or any other meaty white fish.

Ingredients

500ml Moroccan marinade (below)
6 chicken breasts, diced large
1 large onion, diced
100g whole almonds
100g raisins
100g dates, roughly chopped
250ml chicken stock (p.99)
large handful fresh coriander, finely chopped
olive oil
salt and freshly ground black pepper


Ingredients for the marinade, makes 800ml

200ml white wine vinegar
300ml runny honey
125ml fresh lemon juice
1 teaspoon peeled and grated fresh ginger
1 small red chilli, seeds removed and finely sliced
1 clove garlic, crushed
150ml vegetable oil
150ml extra virgin olive oil
2 teaspoons dried mint
2 teaspoons cumin seeds
2 teaspoons fennel seeds
2 teaspoons coriander seeds
2 teaspoons turmeric
1 teaspoon ground cinnamon
1 teaspoon ground cumin
1 teaspoon mild curry powder
½ preserved lemon (washed very well)

Method

Place the marinade ingredients into a blender and blitz until smooth.
Preheat the oven to 190°C.
Place the almonds on a baking tray and bake for about 5 minutes until lightly toasted.
In a large heavy based ovenproof casserole dish with a lid, sweat the onion in a little olive oil on a low heat for about 10 minutes until soft.
Add the diced chicken and Moroccan marinade, along with the toasted almonds, raisins, dates and stock.
Bring to the boil before simmering on a low heat with the lid off for 30 minutes until the chicken is cooked. Otherwise, place in the oven at 160°C with the lid on for the same amount of time.
Season and sprinkle with the coriander to serve.

## THAI GREEN CURRY
for 6

Rich and fragrant, serve this curry with steamed basmati rice and pak choi. It can be made in advance and is quick and easy to reheat making it a perfect post-theatre supper dish.

Ingredients

6 chicken breasts, diced large
1 large onion, finely sliced
3 spring onions, finely sliced
1 clove garlic, crushed
1 lemongrass stalk, outer hard leaves removed and soft centre cut into 1cm pieces
½ lime, skin and pith removed
100ml sweet chilli sauce

1 teaspoon peeled and grated fresh ginger
2 tins full fat coconut milk
30ml sesame oil
1 heaped teaspoon good quality Thai green curry paste
1 teaspoon fish sauce
½ teaspoon ground coriander
¼ teaspoon ground cumin
vegetable oil
salt

Ingredients to add just before serving

100g sugar snap peas, sliced in half lengthways
100g bean sprouts
juice of 1 lime
125ml sweet chilli sauce
1 teaspoon sesame oil
1 teaspoon caster sugar
1 teaspoon fish sauce
small handful fresh mint
small handful fresh basil
large handful fresh coriander
pinch white pepper

Method

In a heavy based ovenproof casserole dish with a lid, sweat the diced onion in a little vegetable oil on a low heat for 10 minutes until soft and translucent. Using a food processor, blend the spring onions, garlic, lemongrass, lime, sweet chilli sauce, ginger, sesame oil, curry paste, fish sauce, ground coriander and ground cumin.
Add this mix to the saucepan and fry for about 5 minutes until fragrant.
Turn up the heat and add the diced chicken to the saucepan to lightly seal the meat. Do not brown the edges of the chicken as this will affect the colour of the curry.

Add the coconut milk and bring to the boil before simmering on a low heat with the lid off for 30 minutes until the chicken is cooked. Otherwise, place in the oven at 160°C with the lid on for the same amount of time.

Meanwhile, place the lime juice, sweet chilli sauce, sesame oil, sugar, fish sauce, mint, basil, coriander and white pepper into a food processor and blend until smooth. Set aside.

When the curry is ready, add this paste, along with the sliced sugar snap peas and bean shoots. Simmer gently on the hob until piping hot before serving.

# COQ AU VIN
## for 6

A classic Finns dish, cook this recipe the night before needed. Allowing it to sit in the fridge overnight allows the chicken to fully absorb the flavour of the sauce. This freezes well.

Ingredients

6 chicken thighs, skin on
6 chicken legs, skin on
500ml red wine
500ml chicken stock (p.99)
200g streaky bacon
250g button mushrooms
12 baby onions, peeled
olive oil
salt and freshly ground black pepper

Method

Preheat the oven to 180°C.
In a large heavy based oven proof casserole dish with a lid, heat a large tablespoon of olive oil.

In batches, brown the chicken until the skin is golden and set aside.

Once all the chicken has been browned, return it to the casserole dish and cover with the red wine and chicken stock. Cover with the lid and place in the oven for 40 minutes.

Meanwhile, in a heavy based pan, fry the bacon until crispy. Do not add oil as the fat from the bacon will be sufficient.

Remove with a slotted spoon and place on kitchen paper.

Fry the mushrooms until golden. Once cooked, remove and reserve with the bacon.

Add the baby onions, along with a little olive oil to the pan and sauté until golden brown. Once cooked, remove and add to the bacon and mushrooms.

Take the casserole out of the oven, remove the chicken from the sauce and set aside.

Skim the excess fat from the sauce.

Return to the hob and bring to the boil. Allow to reduce by half.

Add the bacon, mushrooms and baby onions to the sauce, season, and replace the chicken. At this stage it is ready to serve. However, it best to leave the casserole to cool before refrigerating and serving the following day so that all of the flavours infuse.

## POUSSIN STUFFED WITH COURGETTES, APRICOTS & PINE NUTS
### for 6

A poussin is simply a young chicken, about 4–6 weeks old. Weighing just under 500g, one poussin is perfect for a single serving. It is best to soak the dried apricots in boiling water or chicken stock for 2 hours or even overnight – easy to forget but makes such a difference. This recipe works well with the quinoa, wild rice and lentil salad on p.176, or, for a special Sunday roast, the assortment of roasted root vegetables on p.187.

Ingredients

6 poussin
100g unsalted butter
1 large onion, sliced
1 large carrot, quartered
500ml chicken stock (p.99)
300ml white wine
handful fresh parsley, roughly chopped
salt and freshly ground black pepper

Ingredients for the stuffing

250g dried apricots, roughly chopped and soaked in boiling water or chicken
stock for at least 2 hours
500g courgettes, grated
40g pine nuts, roughly chopped
250ml full fat natural yoghurt
3 sprigs of fresh thyme, leaves picked

Method

Preheat the oven to 180°C.
In a bowl, mix the stuffing ingredients together and season with salt and
freshly ground black pepper.
Place the onion and carrot in a roasting tray.
Clean the poussin, removing any string used to tie up the legs.
Stuff each poussin cavity with the apricot, courgette and pine nut stuffing.
Place the birds on top of the carrot and onions and add half of the stock and
all of the wine.
Place a knob of butter on top of each bird, season and place them in the oven
for 20–25 minutes until the skin is crispy and the juices of the bird run clear.
Remove from the oven and place the birds on a serving tray, cover in foil and
allow to rest, reserving the cooking juices for the sauce.
Use a wooden spoon to scrape all the meaty juices, roasted carrot and onion

off the bottom of the roasting tray. Transfer to a saucepan and add the remaining stock.

Reduce the sauce for 5 minutes. Season and strain before serving with the poussin.

# GUINEA FOWL WITH PROSCIUTTO & MADEIRA
for 6

In the early years, I became glad of the support of Lesley Maiden who died aged 103 after a life that had spanned three centuries. Always urging me to come and have "forty winks" on her spare bed at her house in Sprimont Place, I went round at 3pm for a short break and a quick rest one Thursday. I was greeted by a bottle of Madeira and a packet of cigarettes – in her view the secret to reaching 100 without a stick. When I asked her the greatest difference between her early life and later years, thinking she might talk about cobbled streets and transport, she replied the changing face of job security and the demise of service in the true sense of the word. In her day, a job well done was a job for life. You were not at the mercy of takeovers and restructuring. You worked your way up through hard graft, not careful positioning. The pursuit of excessive reward, in her observation, had been very divisive to family life. It was Lesley Maiden who came to the rescue when a last minute order for twelve portions of this recipe came in. We had no Madeira but I remembered the bottle, ever present on her table. Through Mrs Maiden and the great characters like her who have been the back bone of Finns through the years, I am reminded of the many changing scenes of life.

Ingredients

6 guinea fowl supremes, skin on
6 slices prosciutto
1 medium onion, diced
1 medium carrot, grated

2 medium sticks of celery, sliced
6 fresh sage leaves
250ml Madeira
250ml vegetable stock (p.98)
350ml double cream
olive oil
salt and freshly ground black pepper

Method

Preheat the oven to 180°C.
Trim the sinew and fat from each supreme.
Press a sage leaf into each piece of guinea fowl and wrap each breast in a slice of prosciutto.
In a large heavy based saucepan, heat a little olive oil.
Sear the guinea fowl in small batches in the hot fat so that each breast browns and seals before removing and placing on a roasting tray.
Deglaze the pan with the Madeira and reduce for 3 minutes before adding the vegetable stock. Simmer for 5 minutes.
Pour the sauce over the guinea fowl and roast for 25 minutes.
In a frying pan, sweat the onion in a little olive oil on a low heat for 10 minutes until soft and translucent.
Add the carrots and the celery. Sweat for a further 5 minutes.
Add the cream and reduce for a further 10 minutes, seasoning well.
Remove the fowl from the oven and place on a serving dish, reserving the cooking juices for the sauce. Allow to rest for 10 minutes, covering the supremes in foil so that they stay warm.
Add the cooking juices to the creamy sauce and combine well. Strain before serving with the guinea fowl.

# Pheasant in Calvados Cream
## with Roasted Apples
for 6

This is a great alternative to a traditional pheasant casserole. The best apples to accompany are Braeburn or Cox. Whichever apple you go for, make sure it is an eating apple and not a cooking one. This works very well with the cabbage and pancetta recipe on page 186.

Ingredients

3 plump pheasants, quartered (ask your butcher to quarter them for you)
2 medium onions, diced
2 cloves garlic, crushed
4 eating apples, sliced
25g unsalted butter
25g caster sugar
150ml Calvados
1 pint good apple juice
500ml chicken stock (p.99)
500ml double cream
vegetable oil
salt and freshly ground black pepper

Method

Preheat the oven to 180°C.
Place the apple slices in a roasting tray, dot with the butter and scatter with the sugar.
Roast for 15 minutes, until caramelised.
In a large heavy oven proof casserole dish with a lid, heat a little vegetable oil and brown the pheasant quarters in batches before removing and setting aside.
Deglaze the pan with the calvados and use a wooden spoon to scrape up all the meaty juices on the bottom of the casserole dish.

Return the pheasants to the casserole dish and add the apple juice and chicken stock.

With the lid on, place the casserole dish in the oven. Cook for 40 minutes.

Remove from the oven, take the pheasant out of its cooking juices and allow to cool. Pour the cooking juices into a jug and reserve.

In the now empty casserole dish, sweat the onions in a little olive oil on a low heat for about 10 minutes until soft and translucent. Add the garlic and sweat for a further 5 minutes.

Pour the reserved sauce back into the casserole dish.

Bring to the boil and reduce the mixture by half.

Add the cream and continue to reduce the sauce until it is thick.

Shred the pheasant from the carcasses and discard the bones. Add to the sauce and season with salt and freshly ground black pepper. Slowly reheat the casserole until piping hot and serve garnished with the roasted apple slices.

# Meat

*Give them great meals of beef and iron and steel,*
*they will eat like wolves and fight like devils.*
Henry V
WILLIAM SHAKESPEARE

Boeuf Bourguignon
Beef Curry
Oriental Beef Fillet
Burgundy Beef with Mushrooms and Horseradish Dumplings
Lamb Shanks with Redcurrants and Rosemary
Minted Lamb Casserole
Lamb Tagine
Spiced Lamb Skewers
Veal Blanquette
Veal Clementine
Veal Saltimbocca with Madeira Sauce
Pork Tenderloin with Creamy Mushrooms
Spiced Pork and Pistachio Balls
Honey and Mustard Sausages

Many of these dishes are casseroles and for three decades we have been asked to make them time and time again. For dinner parties, family suppers and weekend house parties, they are completely dependable and utterly delicious. The portions are generous but any leftovers will freeze very well. The slow cooked nature of these casseroles means that they benefit from being cooked up to 2 days in advance of eating.

# Boeuf Bourguignon
for 6 to 8

We have a customer who orders this every week during the winter months and basks in her husband's praises. This dish is delicious on a bed of buttered tagliatelle or with creamy mash (see the recipe on p. 126) with some steamed French beans or roasted carrots.

Ingredients

1.5kg stewing beef, in 2cm square chunks
250g streaky bacon, chopped into lardons
1 large onion, finely sliced
2 cloves garlic, crushed
250g chestnut mushrooms, quartered
450ml red wine
500ml beef stock (p.100)
small knob of unsalted butter
1 bouquet garni of 1 bay leaf, 3 sprigs of fresh rosemary, 5 sprigs of fresh thyme, small handful of fresh parsley
vegetable oil
salt and freshly ground black pepper

Method

In a large heavy based ovenproof casserole dish with a lid, fry the bacon until crispy. Remove with a slotted spoon and allow to rest on kitchen paper.
Sweat the onion in the same casserole dish on a low heat for about 10 minutes until soft and translucent. Add the garlic and sweat for a further 5 minutes. Remove and reserve.
Add a tablespoon of vegetable oil to the casserole dish and turn up the heat. Add the beef and brown the meat.
Return the bacon, onion and garlic to the pan, cover with the red wine, beef stock and add the bouquet garni.
Season and bring to the boil before simmering on a low heat with the lid off for 1½ – 2 hours until the beef is tender. Otherwise, place in the oven at

160°c with the lid on for the same amount of time.

Meanwhile, fry the mushrooms in a little olive oil until golden brown. When the casserole is ready, remove from the heat and add the mushrooms. Adjust the seasoning before serving.

## BEEF CURRY
### for 6 to 8

Colette introduced this South African recipe many years ago. The Robert family have been cooking and enjoying this curry for two generations. Many of our customers order it in large quantities to stock their freezers in case of a surprise visit from a hoard of ravenous teenagers back from school.

Ingredients

1.5kg stewing beef, in 2cm square chunks
1 medium onion, diced
1 clove garlic, crushed
500ml beef stock (p.100)
1 litre tomato juice
2 tablespoons mild curry powder
1 heaped teaspoon turmeric
1 heaped teaspoon ground coriander
1 heaped teaspoon ground cumin
1 heaped teaspoon cayenne pepper
1 heaped teaspoon paprika
1 teaspoon peeled and grated fresh ginger
½ teaspoon fenugreek powder
2 lemongrass stalks, outer leaves removed and soft centre finely chopped
1 small red chilli, seeds removed and finely sliced
500g washed spinach leaves
400g cooked chickpeas
handful fresh coriander, finely chopped
vegetable oil
salt and freshly ground black pepper

Method

In a large heavy based ovenproof casserole dish with a lid, sweat the onion in a little vegetable oil on a low heat for about 10 minutes until soft and translucent.

Add the garlic, chilli, ginger and lemongrass and cook for a further 3–5 minutes.

Add the dry spices and cook for a further 3–5 minutes on a low heat until fragrant.

Turn up the heat, add the beef and brown the meat.

Add the stock and tomato juice and bring to the boil before simmering on a low heat with the lid off for 1½ – 2 hours until the beef is tender. Otherwise, place in the oven at 160°c with the lid on for the same amount of time.

Remove from the heat, add the chickpeas and spinach and stir the curry well. Sprinkle with freshly chopped coriander, season and serve.

# ORIENTAL BEEF FILLET
### for 8 to 10

As with all our meat dishes, the quality of the beef is of paramount importance for this recipe. A great favourite for celebrations and buffets, serve with a selection of salads and warm new potatoes.

Ingredients for the beef

1.2kg beef fillet, trimmed of sinew and fat
1 bunch spring onions, finely sliced
1 large red pepper, seeds removed and finely diced
vegetable oil

Ingredients for the marinade and sauce

1–2 small red chillis, depending on how much spice you like
1 clove garlic, crushed

1 lemongrass stalk, outer hard leaves removed and soft centre cut into 1cm pieces
250ml dark soy sauce
170ml sesame oil
170ml brown rice vinegar
125ml sweet chilli sauce
70ml fish sauce
70ml vegetable oil
70ml fresh lime juice
70g brown sugar
1 teaspoon Chinese five spice

Method the night before

Use a blender or a food processor to blitz the ingredients for the marinade together.
Cover the beef in the sauce and allow to marinate in the fridge overnight.

Method on the day

Preheat the oven to 180°C.
Allow the beef to come to room temperature.
Remove the meat from the marinade and dab dry with kitchen paper. Reserve the marinade for later use.
Heat a large heavy based frying pan with a little vegetable oil until smoking hot.
Sear the meat on all sides.
Remove the beef from the pan and place in a roasting tray.
Cook in the oven for 25–30 minutes (rare).
Remove from the oven and allow to cool.
Place the reserved marinade in a saucepan, bring to the boil before lowering the heat and reducing for about 10 minutes until thickened.
Mix the spring onions and peppers together.
Once cooled, slice the beef into 1cm slices and place on a large platter, garnishing with the spring onions and peppers. Serve with the marinade on the side.

# Burgundy Beef with Mushrooms & Horseradish Dumplings
### for 6 to 8

This old-fashioned recipe is one for the long, cold winter nights. A favourite at shoot lunches, it can be prepared well in advance and reheated when needed. The dumplings make this a substantial dish and served with roasted root vegetables, it is all the more so.

Ingredients for the beef

1.5kg stewing beef, in 2cm square chunks
1 large onion, sliced
2 medium carrots, peeled and sliced
2 medium stalks of celery, sliced
450g button mushrooms
250ml Burgundy wine
5 whole black peppercorns
1 bouquet garni of 1 bay leaf, 4 parsley stalks, 4 sprigs of thyme and 3 tarragon stalks
600ml beef stock (p. 100)
1 teaspoon tomato purée
vegetable oil
salt and freshly ground black pepper

Ingredients for the dumplings

450g plain white flour
100g frozen unsalted butter
2 tablespoons horseradish sauce
375ml full fat natural yoghurt
1 level teaspoon bicarbonate of soda
1 level teaspoon salt

The night before

Place the beef, red wine, onion, carrots, celery, bouquet garni and peppercorns into a bowl and leave to marinate in the fridge overnight.

On the day

Method to make the dumplings

Sieve the flour, bicarbonate of soda and salt into a bowl.                    .
Grate the frozen butter into the bowl and rub with the flour until the mixture resembles the consistency of breadcrumbs.
Add the milk and horseradish and knead the mixture to make a dough.
Roll into small balls, about 2cm in diameter.

Method to make the casserole

Preheat the oven to 160°C.
Remove the marinating meat from the fridge and allow to come to room temperature.
Take the meat out of the marinade and dab dry on kitchen paper. Pass the marinade through a sieve and reserve.
Heat a little vegetable oil in a large heavy based ovenproof casserole dish with a lid.
Dust the beef with 1 tablespoon of plain white flour and fry in small batches, remove each batch of browned meat with a slotted spoon and allow to rest on kitchen paper.
Deglaze the pan with a ladle full of the marinade and use a wooden spoon to scrape up all the meaty juices from the bottom. Add the reserved meat, the rest of the marinade, stock and tomato purée to the casserole dish.
Bring to the boil before placing in the oven for 1½ hours with the lid on.
Meanwhile, in a lightly oiled pan, fry the mushrooms until golden.
After 1½ hours, remove the casserole from the oven, and stir in the mushrooms. Season with salt and freshly ground black pepper before adding the dumplings to the top and returning to the oven to steam, lid on, for a

further 25 minutes. In order to make the dumplings crispy and scone-like, remove the lid, raise the oven temperature to 220°C, and bake the tops for a further 10–15 minutes.

# LAMB SHANKS
## WITH REDCURRANTS & ROSEMARY
### for 6

Lamb shanks were once spurned in favour of more expensive cuts of meat but they are full of flavour and slow cooked until the meat falls away from the bone. This dish can be cooked well in advance. Each shank will serve one person generously.

Ingredients

6 lamb shanks
3 punnets redcurrants
500ml beef stock (p.100)
500ml red wine
3 medium carrots, diced
3 medium celery stalks, diced
5 stalks rosemary
150g redcurrant jelly
vegetable oil
salt and freshly ground black pepper

Method

Preheat the oven to 180°C.
In a large heavy based ovenproof casserole dish with a lid, heat 2 tablespoons of vegetable oil.
Brown the lamb shanks on all sides and set aside.
In the same casserole dish, sweat the diced vegetables on a low heat for about 10 minutes until soft.

Return the lamb to the dish and pour over the stock, wine and redcurrant jelly. Add the rosemary stalks.

Bring to the boil before placing in the oven for 1½ – 2 hours with the lid on, by which time the meat should be incredibly tender and almost falling off the bone.

Remove the lamb shanks from the sauce and reserve. Strain the sauce into a jug and discard the vegetables (optional). Return the lamb to the casserole dish and pour the sauce over the top.

Season with salt and freshly ground black pepper before garnishing with redcurrants.

## MINTED LAMB CASSEROLE
### for 6 to 8

Mint and lamb are a natural pairing and fresh baby vegetables whole, with the tops on, can be added to the casserole – baby carrots, baby turnips, and baby new potatoes.

Ingredients

1.5kg lamb leg, in 2cm square chunks
1 large onion, diced
1 tablespoon mint sauce
500ml good red wine
250ml beef stock (p.100)
1 bunch fresh mint, chopped
vegetable oil
salt and freshly ground black pepper

Method

In a large heavy based ovenproof casserole dish with a lid, sweat the onion in a tablespoon of vegetable oil on a low heat for about 10 minutes until soft and translucent.

Turn up the heat and add the diced lamb to brown the meat before pouring in the mint sauce, red wine and stock.

Bring to the boil before simmering on a low heat with the lid off for 1 ½ – 2 hours until the lamb is tender. Otherwise, place in the oven at 160°C with the lid on for the same amount of time.

Add the freshly chopped mint just before serving and season well.

# LAMB TAGINE
### for 6 to 8

Milly and Harry chose this delicious, lightly spiced tagine as their wedding dinner. There was no need to worry about its being ruined if speeches ran over as the flavours intensify the longer it is left. Milly was married in 2010; photographs of her wedding decorate the shop.

Ingredients

1.5kg lamb leg, in 2cm square chunks
1 large onion, diced
1 red chilli, seeds removed and finely chopped
1 clove garlic, crushed
1 teaspoon peeled and grated fresh ginger
1 tablespoon ground coriander
1 tablespoon ground cumin
1 tablespoon paprika
1 heaped teaspoon turmeric
1 teaspoon cinnamon
¼ teaspoon cayenne pepper
1 tin of best quality chopped plum tomatoes
1 litre shop bought tomato juice
500ml beef stock (p.100)
olive oil
salt and freshly ground black pepper

Method

In a large heavy based oven proof casserole dish with a lid, sauté the onion in a little olive oil until golden brown.
Add the garlic and ginger. Cook for 2–3 minutes.
Add the dry spices and fry for a further 3–5 minutes on a low heat, until the spices become aromatic.
Turn up the heat, add the lamb and brown the meat.
Add the tomatoes, tomato juice and stock and season well.
Bring to the boil before simmering on a low heat with the lid off for 1 ½ hours until the lamb is tender. Otherwise, place in the oven at 160°C with the lid on for the same amount of time.

## SPICED LAMB SKEWERS
for 6

Quick and simple, these skewers are great for BBQs. Serve with salads, baked potatoes and sour cream with diced cucumber and fresh mint. Wooden skewers need to be soaked in water before grilling.

Ingredients

600g lamb, preferably leg, cut into 2cm cubes
2 yellow peppers, seeds removed and cut into 2cm squares
2 tablespoons extra virgin olive oil
zest of 1 lemon
1 teaspoon paprika
1 teaspoon cayenne pepper
1 teaspoon fresh coriander, finely chopped
salt and freshly ground black pepper

Method

In a large bowl, mix the lamb and peppers with the lemon zest, spices, herbs and extra virgin olive oil.

Slide alternate pieces of lamb and peppers onto skewers and griddle on a hot griddle pan or BBQ for about 5 minutes or longer if you prefer the lamb well done.

## Veal Blanquette
### for 6 to 8

A much loved Finns recipe, this is another dish that can be made well in advance. Many of our customers buy it to take to the country at the weekend to serve when their guests arrive on a Friday evening.

Ingredients

1.5kg veal, in 2cm square chunks
300g chestnut mushrooms, quartered
2 large leeks, finely sliced
1 medium onion, diced
1 clove garlic, crushed
500ml beef stock (p.100)
250ml dry white wine
200ml whipping cream
handful fresh sage leaves, finely chopped
olive oil
salt and freshly ground black pepper

Method

In a large heavy based oven proof casserole dish with a lid, melt a large knob of butter and sweat the leeks on a low heat until soft, seasoning with salt and pepper. Remove the leeks from the pan and set aside for later use.

Turn up the heat and sauté the mushrooms until golden brown. Remove and reserve with the leeks.

Add the onion and sweat in a little olive oil on a low heat for about 10 minutes until soft and translucent.

Add the garlic and sage and fry for a further 2 minutes.

Turn up the heat, add the diced veal and brown the meat.

Add the stock, white wine, half the leeks and half the mushrooms.

Bring to the boil before simmering on a low heat with the lid off for 1½ – 2 hours until the veal is tender. Otherwise, place in the oven at 160°C with the lid on for the same amount of time.

Remove the casserole from the heat and separate the veal and clementines from the sauce using a slotted spoon. Set aside.

Add the cream to the sauce and place on the hob on a high heat. Reduce until thickened.

Return the meat to the sauce and season. Garnish with the remaining leeks and mushrooms to serve.


# VEAL CLEMENTINE
## for 6 to 8

One of my favourite dinner party dishes, the tartness of clementine zest works well with the sweetness of the veal.

Ingredients

1.5kg veal, in 2cm square chunks
2 medium onions, diced
handful fresh sage leaves, finely chopped
1 litre beef stock (p.100)
500ml dry white wine
50ml brandy
5 clementines, cut into wedges of 6 with the skin left on
1 tablespoon caster sugar
olive oil
salt and freshly ground black pepper

Method

In a large heavy based ovenproof casserole dish with a lid, sweat the onions in a little olive oil on a low heat for 10 minutes until soft and translucent. Add the sugar and the sage and fry for a further 4 minutes.
Turn up the heat, add the veal to the sage and onion and brown the meat. Remove the contents of the pan and set aside.
Pour the brandy and white wine into the still hot casserole dish and use a wooden spoon to scrape all the meaty juices from the bottom of the pan.
Return the meat to the dish, add the stock and clementines and bring to the boil before simmering on a low heat with the lid off for 1½ – 2 hours until the veal is tender. Otherwise, place in the oven at 160°C with the lid on for the same amount of time.
Remove the casserole from the heat and separate the veal from the sauce using a slotted spoon. Set aside.
Place the casserole dish on the hob and reduce the sauce by half.
Return the meat to the sauce and season.

# VEAL SALTIMBOCCA
## WITH MADEIRA SAUCE
for 6

These delicious parcels can be served with oven roasted new potatoes (p. 184) and fennel, mushrooms and courgettes (p. 180). This dish can be prepared in advance and finished in the oven shortly before serving.

Ingredients

6 veal escalopes
6 slices prosciutto or Parma ham
12 sage leaves
1 large onion, diced
1 large carrot, grated

2 medium sticks of celery, sliced
280ml double cream
100ml Madeira
olive oil
salt and freshly ground black pepper

Method

Preheat the oven to 180°c.
Place a sage leaf in the centre of each piece of veal and fold the escalope in half. Place another sage leaf on top of the veal and wrap the meat in a slice of prosciutto.
In a large heavy based frying pan, heat a little olive oil.
Brown each escalope in the hot fat before removing to an oven proof dish.
In the same pan, sweat the onion in a little olive oil on a low heat for 10 minutes, until soft and translucent.
Add the carrots and the celery. Cook for a further 5 minutes.
Deglaze the pan with the Madeira and cook for a further 2 minutes.
Add the cream and simmer for 10 minutes. Strain into a jug and discard the vegetables.
Pour the strained sauce over the veal. At this stage, you can place the veal in the fridge and finish cooking it later.
When you are ready to serve bring the veal up to room temperature and put the veal dish in the oven, covered, for 20 minutes, until the meat is cooked through.

# PORK TENDERLOIN
# WITH CREAMY MUSHROOMS
for 6

This rich dish is perfect during the gloomy, cold days of winter. Serve with plenty of mashed potato and the cabbage and pancetta recipe on p. 186. It can be made in advance and reheated.

Ingredients

3 pork tenderloins, trimmed of sinew and fat
500g mixture of wild mushrooms
1 medium onion, finely diced
1 clove garlic, crushed
500ml double cream
250ml white wine
250ml vegetable stock (p.98)
2 sprigs of fresh thyme, leaves picked
olive oil
salt and freshly ground black pepper

Method

Preheat the oven to 180°c.
Rub the pork with olive oil, salt and freshly ground black pepper.
Heat a frying pan until smoking hot.
Place the pork in the pan and sear the meat.
Remove to an oven proof dish.
In a large frying pan, sweat the onion in a little olive oil on a low heat for about 10 minutes until soft and translucent. Add the garlic, mushrooms and thyme leaves and fry for a further 5 minutes.
Add the cream, white wine and vegetable stock to the onion, garlic and mushrooms. Turn up the heat, reduce the sauce by 1/3 and season.
Pour the sauce over the meat. At this stage, you can place the pork in the fridge and finish cooking it later.
When you are ready to serve, bring the pork up to room temperature and put in the oven, covered, for 25–30 minutes, until the meat is cooked through.

# SPICED PORK & PISTACHIO BALLS
## for 6

These pork balls can be made large for supper or small for a canapé. Serve with sweet chilli sauce, rice and the spinach and roasted pepper recipe on p. 183.

Ingredients for the pork mix

1 kg pork mince
30g pistachios, roughly chopped
3 spring onions, finely sliced
1 egg
50g fresh white breadcrumbs
2 tablespoons sweet chilli sauce
1 tablespoon rice vinegar
1 teaspoon fish sauce
1 teaspoon sesame oil
1 teaspoon brown sugar
¼ teaspoon Chinese five spice
1 small bunch fresh coriander, roughly chopped
salt and freshly ground black pepper
2 tablespoons of vegetable oil to seal

Ingredients for the spice mix

1 lemongrass stalk, outer hard leaves removed and soft centre cut into 1 cm pieces
small bunch fresh coriander
small bunch fresh mint
½ lime, peeled and pith removed
½ small onion
1 teaspoon cumin seeds
1 teaspoon coriander seeds
1 teaspoon turmeric

1 tablespoon peeled and grated fresh ginger
1 green chilli, seeds removed and finely sliced

Method

Preheat the oven to 180°C.
In a food processor, blend the ingredients for the spice mix.
In a large bowl, combine the ingredients for the pork mix.
Mix the spice mix into the pork mix.
Form the pork mixture into 110g balls.
In a smoking hot frying pan, heat 1 tablespoon of vegetable oil.
Add the pork balls a few at a time and seal them on all sides until golden brown. Keep the pan lightly oiled and smoking hot for each batch.
Place on a baking tray and bake for 10–15 minutes until cooked through.

# Sticky Honey & Mustard Sausages
for 6 to 8

At Finns, we bake many strings of these sausages daily. Hot or cold, they are a perennial favourite and can be made using cocktail sausages for a party. They are extremely sticky so line your baking tray properly to avoid a day of laborious washing up. If you are going to eat them cold, separate them and move them to a serving dish as soon as you remove them from the oven otherwise they will stick together.

Ingredients

12–16 sausages
6 tablespoons runny honey
4 tablespoons wholegrain mustard

Method

Preheat the oven to 190°C.
Line a roasting tray with tin foil and then greaseproof paper.
In a jug, use a fork to mix the honey and mustard together.
Place the sausages in the roasting tray.
Pour the honey and mustard over the sausages.
Bake for 30 minutes before turning the sausages over, making sure the entire sausage is coated with the honey and mustard.
Bake for a further 15 minutes until the sausages are cooked through, black and sticky. You may need to cook them for a little longer, depending on your oven and the size of the sausages.

# Salads and Vegetables

*Dried peas and beans, being rather on the dull side, much like dull people respond readily to the right contacts.*
IRMA S ROMBAUER

Orzo with Grated Courgette, Parmesan and Lemon
Mixed Rice with Roasted Vegetables
Marinated Chickpeas with Minted Yoghurt and Aubergines
Lentils with Sun-blushed Tomatoes, Feta and Walnuts
Quinoa, Lentil and Wild Rice Salad
Jewelled Couscous
Beetroot with Pistachio Nut Pesto and Goat's Cheese
Grilled Courgettes with Fennel and Mushrooms
Broccoli with Preserved Lemon and Mixed Seeds
Broad Bean, Edamame, Pea, Radish and Mozzarella Salad
Spinach with Roasted Red Onion and Peppers
Roasted New Potatoes with Rosemary and Garlic
Parsnip and Carrot Purée
Savoy Cabbage and Pancetta
Roasted Root Vegetables

# ORZO WITH GRATED COURGETTE, PARMESAN & LEMON

## for 6

Despite looking a lot like rice, orzo is a type of pasta. This is one of Colette's favourite recipes. When cooking it at home, she adds fresh prawns turning the side dish into a summer main course. Make sure you use lemon zest rather than lemon juice to flavour the pasta – lemon juice turns the courgettes brown and ruins the pretty greens and yellows of this dish.

Ingredients

500g orzo pasta
3 medium courgettes, grated
200g parmesan, shaved
1 small red chilli, seeds removed and finely sliced
2 cloves garlic, crushed
zest of 2 lemons
extra virgin olive oil
salt and freshly ground black pepper

Method

Bring a large pan of salted water to the boil. Add the orzo pasta and cook until al dente.
Drain and toss in extra virgin olive oil before placing in a serving dish.
In a frying pan, heat a tablespoon of olive oil and sauté the garlic, chilli and grated courgettes for about 8 minutes and remove to the serving dish.
Mix thoroughly, adding the lemon zest, salt, freshly ground black pepper and extra virgin olive oil to taste.
Scatter with the shaved parmesan to serve.

# MIXED RICE WITH ROASTED VEGETABLES
for 6

This works well served hot with all casseroles and equally well as a summer salad.

Ingredients

150g wild rice
150g white rice
150g brown rice
2 red peppers, cut into medium squares
2 yellow peppers, cut into medium squares
2 large courgettes, cut into 1cm slices and then quartered
olive oil
extra virgin olive oil
salt and freshly ground black pepper

Method

Preheat the oven to 200°C.
Place the courgettes and peppers on a large baking tray, using two baking trays if needed. It is important that each vegetable has room to roast. If they are too crowded they will simply steam and go soggy rather than crisp up and caramelise.
Drizzle with olive oil and sprinkle with salt and freshly ground black pepper. Roast for 25 minutes.

Method to cook the different rices

Wash each type of rice separately in cold water. Place the brown and wild rice into one large saucepan, and the white rice separately in another. Cover each in cold water, add a pinch of salt and bring to the boil, before turning down the heat and cooking until tender. Drain and place them all together in a serving dish.

Mix the roasted vegetables with the rice, season with salt and freshly ground black pepper, drizzle with extra virgin olive oil and garnish with freshly chopped basil leaves.

## MARINATED CHICKPEAS WITH MINTED YOGHURT & AUBERGINES
### for 6

This is a wonderful vegetarian main course. The combination of lightly spiced chickpeas, cool, creamy yoghurt and fried aubergines makes for a satisfying dish that even the most carnivorous will enjoy as a meal in itself. This works very well when served with pitta bread and a crunchy green salad.

It is impossible to make small quantities of the Moroccan marinade without compromising the recipe. Make the marinade recipe below but only use the amount quoted in the ingredients for the chickpeas. Reserve the remainder for another day. It will keep in the fridge for 2 weeks. It is used in the Moroccan chicken recipe on page 140 and works well as a marinade for monkfish or any other meaty white fish.

Ingredients

250ml Moroccan marinade (below)
800g cooked chickpeas
2 aubergines, stalk removed and cut into 1 cm cubes
1 large onion, finely diced
100g full fat natural yoghurt
olive oil
vegetable oil
small bunch fresh mint, finely chopped
salt and freshly ground black pepper

Ingredients for the marinade, makes 800ml

200ml white wine vinegar
300ml runny honey
125ml fresh lemon juice
1 teaspoon peeled and grated fresh ginger
1 small red chilli, seeds removed and finely sliced
1 clove garlic, crushed
150ml vegetable oil
150ml extra virgin olive oil
2 teaspoons dried mint
2 teaspoons cumin seeds
2 teaspoons fennel seeds
2 teaspoons coriander seeds
2 teaspoons turmeric
1 teaspoon ground cinnamon
1 teaspoon ground cumin
1 teaspoon mild curry powder
½ preserved lemon (washed very well)

Method

Place the marinade ingredients into a blender and blitz until smooth.
In a bowl, mix the yoghurt with the mint leaves, salt and freshly ground black pepper.
In a large frying pan, sweat the onion in a little olive oil on a low heat for about 10 minutes until soft and translucent.
Add the marinade and chickpeas and cook for 5 minutes. Set aside in a serving dish to cool.
Meanwhile, in a large heavy based frying pan, heat 2 tablespoons of vegetable oil and fry the aubergines until golden and crispy. Remove and allow to cool on kitchen paper to absorb the excess oil. Season with salt and freshly ground black pepper.
Cover the chickpeas in the minted yoghurt and top with the fried aubergines.

# LENTILS WITH SUN-BLUSHED TOMATOES, FETA & WALNUTS
### for 6 to 8

This popular salad is best served at room temperature and is often bought to serve with Finns avocado hummus.

Ingredients

300g Puy lentils
100g sun-blushed tomatoes
200g feta cheese, cubed
100g walnuts

Ingredients for the dressing

200ml extra virgin olive oil
juice of 1 lemon
pinch paprika
pinch cayenne pepper
salt

Method

Preheat the oven to 180°C.
Place the nuts on a baking tray and bake for 5 minutes.

Method to cook the lentils

Wash the lentils thoroughly in cold water.
Place in a large saucepan and cover in cold water. Do not add salt as this toughens the skin of the lentils. Bring to the boil before turning down the heat and simmering until tender. Drain.
Place the lentils in a large bowl and mix with the sun-blushed tomatoes, feta and walnuts.
In a jug whisk the oil, lemon, paprika, cayenne pepper and salt together.
Pour over the lentils, mix well and serve.

# Quinoa, Lentil & Wild Rice Salad
## for 6

Colette calls this salad a "big bowl of goodness" and it is one of her favourite dishes. Supremely healthy, the quantities of wild rice, quinoa, couscous and Puy lentils can be altered to suit specific tastes. In the absence of pomegranate seeds, dried cranberries can be used.

Ingredients

150g wild rice
150g quinoa
150g couscous
150g Puy lentils
picked seeds of 1 pomegranate
large handful parsley, finely chopped
large handful coriander, finely chopped
zest of 1 lemon
1 red pepper, seeds removed and diced
100g bean shoots
½ teaspoon ground cumin
handful pecans and walnuts
extra virgin olive oil
salt and freshly ground black pepper

Method

Preheat the oven to 180°C.
Place the nuts on a baking tray and bake for 5 minutes.

Method to cook the wild rice

Wash the rice in cold water and place in a large saucepan. Cover in cold water, add a pinch of salt and bring to the boil, before turning down the heat and cooking until tender. Drain.

Method to cook the quinoa

Wash the quinoa thoroughly in cold water and place in a large saucepan. Cover in cold water, add a pinch of salt and bring to the boil, before turning down the heat and cooking until tender.
Drain.

Method to cook the couscous

Place the couscous in a bowl and drizzle with a tablespoon of extra virgin olive oil. Mix so that each grain is coated.
Cover with boiling water so that the water sits ½cm above the grains.
Cover the bowl with cling film and leave for 10 minutes.
Fluff the couscous with a fork – if you use a spoon, the grains will stick together and form lumps.

Method to cook the lentils

Wash the lentils thoroughly in cold water.
Place in a large saucepan and cover in cold water. Do not add salt as this toughens the skin of the lentils. Bring to the boil before turning down the heat and simmering until tender. Drain.

In a large bowl, mix the pomegranate seeds, herbs, lemon zest, peppers, bean sprouts, cumin and toasted nuts.
Add the cooled pulses and grains.
Mix thoroughly and season well, drizzling with extra virgin olive oil.

## JEWELLED COUSCOUS
### for 6

The beauty of couscous is that it does not need to be served piping hot so you can make it in advance. It is a perfect side dish to the Moroccan chicken on p. 140. It also good with feta cheese crumbled over the top.

Ingredients

500g couscous
100g dried cranberries
picked seeds of 1 pomegranate
handful of parsley, finely chopped
extra virgin olive oil
salt and freshly ground black pepper

Method

Place the couscous in a bowl, drizzle with a tablespoon of extra virgin olive oil and season with salt and pepper. Mix so that each grain is coated.
Cover with boiling water so that the water sits ½cm above the grains.
Cover the bowl with cling film and leave for 10 minutes.
Fluff the couscous with a fork – if you use a spoon, the grains will stick together and form lumps.

Add the cranberries, pomegranate seeds and parsley to the couscous and season. Drizzle with extra virgin olive oil.

# Beetroot with Pistachio Nut Pesto & Goat's Cheese
## for 6

Beetroot is in season from July to January. Their fantastic colour make them a great addition to salads. This recipe is very popular as a vegetarian main course, a first course or a salad. Do not be tempted to blitz the pesto ingredients in a food processor – chopping by hand gives a much better texture to the salad.

Ingredients

12 small summer beetroot, peeled and cut into chunks
150g goat's cheese log, with a rind, cut into 1cm rounds
1 tablespoon runny honey
2 fresh sprigs of thyme, leaves picked
olive oil

Ingredients for the pesto

small bunch each of fresh coriander, parsley and mint leaves, very finely chopped, amounting to about 60g in total
2 spring onions, coarsely chopped
1 clove garlic, crushed
60g pistachios, very finely chopped plus a small handful, unchopped, to garnish
zest and juice of ½ lemon
75ml extra virgin olive oil
salt and freshly ground black pepper

Method to cook the beetroot

Preheat the oven to 180°C.
Place the beetroot in a roasting tray and drizzle with a little olive oil, seasoning with salt and pepper. If the beetroot is not young, add a cup of water to the roasting tray and cover with foil whilst roasting, removing the foil for the final 10 minutes.
Roast for 40 minutes until caramelised and tender.

Method to make the pesto

In a bowl, stir all the ingredients together to form a loose pesto sauce.
Add the pesto to the beetroot and mix together.

Preheat the grill to a high heat.
Lay the goat's cheese onto a baking sheet, drizzle with the olive oil and honey and sprinkle with the fresh thyme. Season with salt and pepper.
Grill for 5 minutes, until slightly golden.

Place the pesto beetroot on a large serving plate, top with the grilled goat's cheese, drizzle with extra virgin olive oil and garnish with the remaining pistachio nuts.

# GRILLED COURGETTES
## WITH FENNEL & MUSHROOMS
for 6

This can be eaten hot or cold. The aniseed notes from the fennel make it a natural pairing with fish. It also works very well served hot with the pork tenderloin with creamy mushrooms on p. 165.

Ingredients

3 large courgettes, cut into thirds and then halved and cut on the diagonal
2 bulbs of fennel, cut into wedges, leaving the root in tact so that it holds together
250g button mushrooms, halved
olive oil
extra virgin olive oil
salt and freshly ground black pepper

Method

Preheat the oven to 200°C.
Place the fennel in a roasting tray, drizzle with olive oil and lightly season.

Roast the fennel for 25 minutes.

Heat a griddle pan until smoking hot and griddle the courgettes for 30 seconds on each side until you can see the griddle lines.

Fry the mushrooms in a little olive oil for about 5 minutes until golden brown.

Mix the vegetables together and add salt and freshly ground black pepper to taste, drizzling with extra virgin olive oil to serve.

# BROCCOLI
## WITH PRESERVED LEMON & MIXED SEEDS
serves 6

Preserved lemon is a popular ingredient in Moroccan cuisine. Lemons, or pieces of lemon, are preserved in a mixture of water, lemon juice and salt and left to ferment for a number of weeks. The rind takes on a very concentrated lemon flavour which is quite tart, without being bitter. It is important to rinse very well otherwise it is too salty. This side dish works very well with salmon. For a vegetarian main course, bake a large chunk of feta or halloumi cheese drizzled with olive oil at 180°C for 20 minutes and serve with penne pasta and the broccoli.

Ingredients

500g broccoli, cut into florets
2 slices of preserved lemon, washed very well and cut into very small cubes
40g of a mixture of seeds: sunflower, pumpkin, linseeds, sesame seeds and poppy seeds
extra virgin olive oil
freshly ground black pepper

Method

Preheat the oven to 180°c.
Place the seeds on a baking tray and bake for 5 minutes.
Steam the broccoli for 3–5 minutes until tender. If serving cold, refresh in iced water.
Remove the broccoli to a large bowl and scatter with the preserved lemon, seeds and freshly ground black pepper.
Mix well, drizzling with extra virgin olive oil.

# Broad Bean, Edamame, Pea, Radish & Mozzarella Salad
### for 6

Katie loves using this recipe as part of a selection of salads when preparing summer picnics and lunches for her friends. The peppery piquancy of the radishes adds an extra dimension of flavour to this recipe as well as making this salad look very vibrant. This salad works really well with the cold lemon and tarragon chicken strips on p.136.

Ingredients

250g edamame beans
250g baby broad beans
250g peas
6 radishes, finely sliced
1 ball of Buffalo mozzarella, torn
2 punnets of pea shoots
extra virgin olive oil
handful fresh parsley, finely chopped
salt and freshly ground black pepper

Method

Bring a pan of salted water to the boil.
Add the edamame beans and boil for 8 minutes. Add the broad beans and boil for a further 5 minutes before adding the peas and boiling for a further 2 minutes.
Drain and refresh in iced water.
Mix the edamame, broad beans and peas with the mozzarella, radishes, parsley, salt and freshly ground black pepper.
Drizzle with extra virgin olive oil and garnish with pea shoots before serving.

# Spinach
## with Roasted Red Onion & Peppers
### for 6

This salad is a healthy accompaniment to a whole host of dishes. At Finns, we often use it as a filling for a quiche too, adding a little goat's cheese to the brightly coloured mixture. 2kg seems like a lot of spinach but it will cook down. This works very well with the spiced pork and pistachio balls on p.167 and the veal saltimbocca on p.164. If you wish to serve this hot, it can be prepared in advance and transferred to an oven proof dish to be reheated when required.

Ingredients

2kg raw spinach
1 yellow pepper, seeds removed and cut into 2cm squares
1 red pepper, seeds removed and cut into 2cm squares
1 red onion, peeled and cut into quarters
½ teaspoon of freshly grated nutmeg
olive oil
salt and freshly ground black pepper

Method

Preheat the oven to 180°C.
Place the peppers on a roasting tray with the onion, using 2 baking trays if needed. It is important that each vegetable has room to roast. If they are too crowded they will simply steam and go soggy. Drizzle with olive oil, season with the nutmeg, salt and freshly ground black pepper.
Roast for 15 minutes.
Put the well washed spinach in a large saucepan and heat gently until wilted. Remove to a colander and allow to cool. Sprinkle with salt and squeeze all the water out.
Mix the spinach with the roasted peppers and onions, season and serve.

# ROASTED NEW POTATOES
## WITH ROSEMARY & GARLIC
for 6

If I had a vegetable garden, the one vegetable I would definitely grow would be new potatoes. Fresh from the ground, they are in a league of their own.

Ingredients

600g new potatoes
4 cloves garlic, skin left on
4 sprigs of rosemary
4 tablespoons olive oil
salt and freshly ground black pepper

Method

Preheat the oven to 200°C.
Line a roasting tray with greaseproof paper.

Place the potatoes into the tray along with the rosemary, garlic, salt, freshly ground black pepper and olive oil. Use a spoon to mix everything together, making sure that the potatoes are coated in oil and seasoning.

Roast for 40 minutes until the potatoes are golden brown, turning the potatoes after 20 minutes.

# Parsnip & Carrot Purée
## for 6

This is a delicious vegetable accompaniment to a Sunday roast. The peelings from the carrots and parsnips can be shallow fried in vegetable oil to make fantastic vegetable crisps to top soups, or serve as pre-dinner nibbles. We receive many orders for our purées throughout the year, especially at Thanksgiving and Christmas.

Ingredients

600g carrots, peeled and cut into 1 inch batons
600g parsnips, peeled, cut into 1 inch batons with the woody centre removed
2 litres vegetable stock (p.98)
150g salted butter
freshly ground black pepper

Method

Place the carrots and parsnips in a saucepan. Cover in the vegetable stock and simmer for 45 minutes.
Remove from the heat and add the butter before blending the mixture with a hand stick blender.
Season with freshly ground black pepper and serve.

# Savoy Cabbage & Pancetta
## for 6

A classic vegetable dish to accompany roasts and casseroles, this dish is a good replacement for Brussel Sprouts at Christmas. We recommend that you buy a block of pancetta rather than the ready sliced variety as it is much more flavoursome and less fatty.

Ingredients

1 large Savoy cabbage
200g pancetta, cubed
20g unsalted butter
salt and freshly ground black pepper

Method

Fry the pancetta until crispy.
Remove from the pan with a slotted spoon and leave to rest on kitchen paper.
Trim the base of the cabbage, remove the core and chop into thin slices. Wash the leaves very well.
In the same pan, melt the butter.
Add the cabbage and fry for about 10 minutes until soft.
Mix the cabbage with the bacon and serve.

# ROASTED ROOT VEGETABLES
for 6

This dish is very popular at Thanksgiving and Christmas, when root vegetables are at their best. Be sure not to use parsnips until after the first frost, otherwise they will be woody and dry rather than sweet and flavoursome. Any leftovers can be made into a chunky soup when added to chicken or vegetable stock.

Ingredients

3 large carrots, peeled and cut into 1 inch batons
½ celeriac, peeled and cut into 1 inch chunks
3 large parsnips, peeled, cut into 1 inch batons with the woody centre removed
1 medium squash, peeled and cut into 1 inch chunks
1 tablespoon runny honey
extra virgin olive oil
small handful of fresh thyme leaves
small handful of fresh sage leaves, roughly chopped
salt and freshly ground black pepper

Method

Preheat the oven to 200°C.
Place the carrots and celeriac onto 1 roasting tray and the parsnips and squash onto another.
Drizzle each tray with extra virgin olive oil, and the parsnips and squash with honey. Season with salt and freshly ground black pepper and scatter with the herbs.
Roast the parsnips and squash for 45 minutes and the carrots and celeriac for 30 minutes until crisp and tender.
Mix the root vegetables together in a large serving bowl. Season well and serve.

# Puddings

*We sliced the fruit in two, holding our halves over a couple of broad leaves so that none of the juice would be lost. It was a good one, thin-skinned and tart beneath its sweetness. I remember how we sucked every drop of the juice, how we rasped the flesh clear of the skin with our teeth, then sucked at what remained until our mouths were bitter and cottony.*
Five Quarters of the Orange – JOANNE HARRIS

Baked Peaches with Brandy & Vanilla and Cinnamon Mascarpone
Plum Compôte
Poached Pears with Pomegranate Seeds
Lemon and Ginger Mousse
Vanilla Panna Cotta with Honey and Figs
Raspberry and Sweet Geranium Jelly
Fig and Pistachio Frangipane Tart
Chocolate Meringue Roulade
Chocolate Bread and Butter Pudding
Good Old-fashioned Apple and Rhubarb Crumble

## BAKED PEACHES WITH BRANDY & VANILLA AND CINNAMON MASCARPONE
for 6

An excellent dinner party pudding. It can be made in advance and warmed before serving. Vanilla mascarpone is very popular at Finns and is delicious served with any crumbles, bread and butter puddings or fruit compôte.

Ingredients

6 peaches, halved, stone removed and skin on
125g unsalted butter
1 tablespoon dark brown soft sugar
100ml brandy
zest and juice of 1 orange

Ingredients for the vanilla mascarpone

350g mascarpone
1 vanilla pod
150g icing sugar, sifted
½ teaspoon ground cinnamon

Method to cook the peaches

Preheat the oven to 180°C.
Line a roasting tray with greaseproof paper and lay the peaches out, flesh side up.
Put a knob of butter into the centre of each peach half.
Sprinkle with brown sugar and orange zest and pour over the brandy and orange juice.
Bake for 30–40 minutes.

Method to make the mascarpone

Use a sharp knife to cut the vanilla pod in half and scrape out the seeds.
Place the vanilla pod seeds, cinnamon, icing sugar and mascarpone into a bowl and mix together using a spatula or wooden spoon.

Serve the warm peaches with the mascarpone and drizzle some of the sauce made from the butter and brandy over each peach.

# PLUM COMPÔTE
makes 6 portions

All our compôtes are bought regularly to serve as a pudding with honeycomb ice-cream or mascarpone. It is also very popular at breakfast time in the shop. I love it with thick Sheep's milk yoghurt, the sugar completely killing the benefit of the healthy yoghurt!

Ingredients

9 plums, halved, stone removed and skin on
2–3 tablespoons demerara sugar (2 for Victoria plums as they are sweeter)
½ vanilla pod or zest 1 orange or 1 teaspoon peeled and grated fresh ginger
100ml water

The night before

Place the plums in a large bowl with the sugar and your choice of flavouring. If you are using vanilla, halve the pod lengthways with a sharp knife and scrape the seeds out. Place both the seeds and the pod into the bowl.
Mix well so that each plum is coated in sugar and flavouring.
Cover in cling film and leave in the fridge overnight.

Method to cook the plums

Preheat the oven to 180°C.
Place the marinated plums in a large baking tray and add the water. Cover with foil and bake for about 30 minutes or until the plums are tender and syrupy. You may need to add extra sugar before serving.

# Poached Pears
## with Pomegranate Seeds
### for 6

This is a good pudding for Christmas, the bright red pomegranate seeds giving it a distinctive festive look. The pears look beautiful served from a large glass bowl. The wine used should be dry and of a reasonably good quality.

Ingredients

6 Conference pears
picked seeds of 2 pomegranates
700ml dry white wine
1 litre water
175g caster sugar
1 strip of thinly pared lemon zest
2 star anise
1 teaspoon peeled and grated fresh ginger
1 teaspoon stem ginger paste (see Notes on p.88)

Method

Cut out a circle of greaseproof paper, the same size as the diameter of your chosen saucepan – you will need a large heavy based one.
Peel the pears, leaving the stalk on.
Place the white wine, water, sugar, lemon zest, star anise, ginger and stem ginger into a saucepan.
Bring to the boil.
Place the pears into the syrup and cook over a low heat, laying the greaseproof paper cut out on top of the syrup. Simmer for 1 hour.
Discard the greaseproof paper and remove the pears from the syrup using a slotted spoon.
Reduce the syrup by one third.
Strain the syrup and serve with the pears, scattering each serving plate with pomegranate seeds.

# Lemon & Ginger Mousse
## for 6 generous portions

This mousse is zesty with a subtle spicy tang. Many of our customers never have a dinner party without it and serve it with Marisa's shortbread. Buying best quality lemon curd rather than using the recipe below is fine in an emergency but the tang and texture is somewhat inferior.

Ingredients for the lemon curd

100g unsalted butter
220g caster sugar
zest and juice of 4 lemons
3 eggs plus 2 yolks, beaten

Ingredients for the mousse

550ml whipping cream
1 dessert spoon stem ginger paste (see Notes on p.88)

Method to make the lemon curd

Place an empty bowl into the fridge to cool. This will hold the lemon curd mixture.
In a heavy based saucepan, melt the butter and the sugar on low heat.
Add the lemon juice and zest.
Add the eggs and continue cooking over a very gentle heat until the mixture coats the back of a spoon. Sieve the mixture into the cold bowl.
Leave to sit in the fridge until completely cool. The mixture will thicken as it cools.

Method to make the mousse

Whip the cream to stiff peaks.
With a metal spoon or plastic spatula, fold in the stem ginger paste.

Add a spoonful of whipped cream to the lemon curd mixture and beat together. Fold this mixture into the cream using a spatula or metal spoon until well combined.

Pour the mousse into a serving bowl and garnish with extra lemon zest.

# Vanilla Panna Cotta with Honey & Figs
## for 6 generous servings

Early Italian recipes for panna cotta used fish bones in place of gelatin and omitted the sugar! This modern recipe is altogether sweeter. It works best when made the day before needed. Berries are a good substitute for the figs, especially slightly tart raspberries.

Ingredients

1 litre double cream
2 vanilla pods
2½ gelatine leaves, each one measuring 11cm by 7cm
125ml whole milk
6 ripe figs
6 tablespoons runny honey
a splash of Marsala or Madeira

Method

Heat 750ml of the cream in a heavy based saucepan.
Add the vanilla pods and bring to the boil.
Reduce the mixture by 1/3, remove from the heat and retrieve the vanilla pods, halving them and scraping the seeds into the reduced cream. Discard the scraped pods.
In a bowl, soak the gelatine in the milk for 15 minutes.
Remove the gelatine with a slotted spoon and reserve for later use.

In a saucepan, heat the milk until boiling. Place the gelatine in the saucepan and stir until dissolved.

Add the milk and gelatine to the cream. Allow to cool.

Whip the remaining cream with the icing sugar.

Fold the whipped cream into the cooled cream, milk and gelatine.

Pour into 6 ramekins or dariole moulds and allow to cool in the fridge for at least 2 hours or overnight.

Preheat the oven to 180°C.

Trim the stalks of the figs and almost cut each fig into quarters, nearly cutting down to the bottom of the fruit. Gently open the fruit out, pinching at the base so that the inside flesh is displayed.

Place in a baking tray and drizzle with the honey and Marsala or Madeira. Cover and bake for 20 minutes.

To turn out the panna cottas, plunge the base of each ramekin or dariole mould into a bowl of boiling water. Remove from the water, put the serving plate on top of the ramekin and invert.

Place a fig by each panna cotta and drizzle with the warm honey juice.

# RASPBERRY & SWEET GERANIUM JELLY
makes 1.5 litres of jelly

The leaves of a sweet geranium plant make a lovely flavouring for this summer jelly. In the absence of sweet geranium, lavender or elderflowers make a good substitute.

Ingredients

1 litre water
500g caster sugar
500g raspberries
3 leaves sweet geranium
12 leaves of gelatine, each one measuring 11cm by 7cm

Method

Place the water, sugar, raspberries and sweet geranium into a large heavy based saucepan.

Bring to the boil before turning down the heat and allowing to simmer for 4–5 minutes, until the sugar has dissolved and the mixture has infused with the sweet geranium.

Remove from the heat and pass the mixture through a sieve. Remove half of the raspberries from the sieve and reserve for later use. Using a wooden spoon, push the remaining raspberries through the sieve so that you retain all the seeds but give the jelly a good colour and flavour.

Place the jelly mixture into the original saucepan with the gelatine leaves. Heat gently until the gelatine has dissolved.

Place the reserved raspberries into the jelly mould(s) and pour the jelly mixture over the top.

Leave to set overnight in the fridge.

# Fig & Pistachio Frangipane Tart
## makes 1 x 30cm tart, enough for 12 generous servings

One of Rosa's favourite recipes, this tart is a truly beautiful end to a summer feast. Sweet and sticky, it is always popular in the Finns café with one of Milly's signature macchiati.

Ingredients

1 quantity of sweet shortcrust pastry at room temperature (p. 110)
1 egg, lightly whisked with which to brush the pastry
220g plain white flour
220g caster sugar
440g ground almonds

4 eggs, plus 1 extra yolk
18 figs, halved
handful pistachios
3 tablespoons runny honey

Method

Preheat the oven to 180°C.
Roll the pastry out and line the tart tin with it. Make sure that the pastry overhangs the edges of the tin about 1 cm as it shrinks whilst it cooks.
Place the pastry into the freezer for 20 minutes.
Remove from the freezer and bake blind for 30 minutes.
Remove the baking beans and brush the pastry with the beaten egg before baking for a further 4 minutes, until golden brown.

Method to make the tart

Preheat the oven to 180°C.
Place the pistachios on a baking tray and cover in a tablespoon of honey, making sure each nut is well coated.
Bake the nuts for 5 minutes.
Turn the temperature of the oven down to 160°C.
Beat together the butter, sugar, almonds and flour.
In a jug, whisk together the eggs before adding them slowly to the butter, almond and flour mix.
Spoon the mix into the tart base.
Lay the figs, flesh side up, around the tart.
Bake for 1½ – 2 hours, until the tart is firm and the figs are slightly caramelised.
Heat the remaining honey in a saucepan and brush it over the tart. Sprinkle with the nuts.

# CHOCOLATE MERINGUE ROULADE
makes 1 roulade, enough for 8 to 10 slices

This pudding is often ordered for a celebration instead of a cake. It is popular with all ages and any combination of berries can be used. The meringue can be made the day before but it is best to roll it on the day.

Ingredients

7 egg whites
400g caster sugar
1 tablespoon cocoa powder, sifted
250ml double cream, whipped
250g raspberries
1 tablespoon icing sugar, sifted
100g dark chocolate, melted
vegetable oil

Method

Preheat the oven to 180°C.
Line a 21cm x 30cm baking tray with tin foil brushed with vegetable oil.
In a very clean and completely dry metal or glass bowl, whisk the egg whites until they form soft peaks.
Add the sugar spoonful by spoonful, continuing to whisk until it forms a glossy mixture.
Using a spatula, fold in the sifted cocoa powder.
Spoon the mixture onto the baking tray and spread out evenly.
Cook for 25 minutes until the meringue is slightly hard on top and beginning to crack. It does not need to be dry throughout like a traditional meringue.
Remove the roulade from the oven and allow to cool.
Cut a large rectangle of greaseproof paper and cover in the icing sugar.
Turn the meringue out onto the greaseproof paper top side down, carefully peeling off the tin foil.

Spread the whipped cream over the sticky meringue base.

Dot the cream with 2/3 of the raspberries and sprinkle with icing sugar.

Using the greaseproof paper as support, roll the roulade starting from the long edge. It will invariably crack but this is part of its charm!

Drizzle the melted chocolate over the roulade and serve with extra raspberries.

## CHOCOLATE BREAD & BUTTER PUDDING
### for 8 to 10

This nursery pudding is a great favourite with adults and children alike. We have many customers who order it for midweek family suppers. It needs to be prepared the day before.

Ingredients

18 slices white bread, crusts removed and quartered into triangles
200g good quality milk chocolate
250g unsalted butter
3 tablespoons drinking chocolate
200g caster sugar
2 tins evaporated milk
2 tablespoons rum
5ml vanilla essence
4 eggs
250ml double cream

Method

Melt the chocolate and butter in a bain-marie.
Whisk in the drinking chocolate and caster sugar.

Allow to cool.

In a large bowl, whisk together the evaporated milk, rum, vanilla essence, eggs and cream.

Stir the 2 mixtures together.

Cover the bottom of a 21cm by 30cm oven proof dish with an 1/8 of the chocolate mixture.

Arrange the bread in layers and pour over 2/3 of the remaining chocolate mixture.

Cover with cling film and allow to stand overnight in the fridge, reserving the remaining chocolate mixture.

Preheat the oven to 180°C.

Pour the reserved custard mixture over the pudding.

Put the oven proof dish into a larger roasting tray and half fill the tray with boiling water.

Bake in the oven for 40–60 minutes. The pudding is ready when it still has a slight wobble and is puffed up and crispy on top.

# GOOD OLD-FASHIONED
# APPLE & RHUBARB CRUMBLE
for 6 people

An absolute autumn-winter classic, this crumble is ordered time and time again. It can be made two days in advance and will work with any seasonal fruit.

Ingredients

50g ground almonds
50g brown sugar
80g plain white flour
30g oats
50g unsalted butter, cold and cubed

6–8 cooking apples, peeled and chopped
4 sticks of rhubarb, cut into 3cm pieces
250g caster sugar
125g unsalted butter
125ml water
1 vanilla pod, split and seeded

Method to cook the fruit

In a large saucepan melt the butter with the sugar.
Add the apples, rhubarb, vanilla pod and seeds and the water.
Cook until soft.
Place the fruit in an ovenproof dish.

Method to make the crumble

Preheat the oven to 180°c.
Rub the cubed butter with the flour until it becomes the consistency of breadcrumbs. Add the remaining ingredients and mix well.
Top the fruit with the mixture and bake for about 25–35 minutes.

# Baking

*There was a silver tea-pot, and a silver kettle with a little spirit-lamp underneath, and a silver cream jug and a covered silver dish full of muffins. There was also hot buttered toast and honey and gentleman's relish and a chocolate cake, a cherry cake, a seed cake and a fruit cake and some tomato sandwiches and pepper and salt and currant bread and butter.*
Vile Bodies – EVELYN WAUGH

Brownies
Victoria Sponge
Finns Carrot Cake
Lemon and Polenta Cake
White Chocolate and Pistachio Cookies
Marisa's Shortbread
Buttermilk Caraway Rusks
"Hi Darling" Muesli

The following recipes have proved some of our most popular over the years, asked for time and time again for children's parties, picnics, elevenses, tea-times and birthdays. In the recipes below, the butter and eggs used are all at room temperature, unless specifically stated otherwise.

## BROWNIES
makes 16 brownies

Ideal for picnics, at Finns we always have a batch of these brownies to hand. Dense and rich, when Katie makes these with her niece, she adds a handful of milk and white chocolate chunks in place of the hazelnuts. They freeze extremely well.

Ingredients

230g unsalted butter
230g dark chocolate
4 eggs
340g caster sugar
110g whole hazelnuts
110g white self-raising flour

Method

Preheat the oven to 180°C.
Line and grease a 21cm x 30cm baking tray.
Melt the chocolate and butter over a bain-marie.
Remove from the heat.
In a large bowl, whisk together the eggs and caster sugar until thick and pale before folding in the chocolate and butter mix.
Sift the flour and fold it into the wet ingredients using a plastic spatula or metal spoon.
Pour the mixture into the baking tray and scatter the hazelnuts on top. During cooking, the hazelnuts will sink into the brownies.
Bake for 35–40 minutes until the mixture begins to pull away from the sides and is firming on top; if you plunge a knife into the centre, it will not come out clean as the mixture is meant to be gooey, even when cooked.
Turn onto a wire rack and allow to cool.
Cut into 16 squares and dust with icing sugar to serve.

## VICTORIA SPONGE
makes 1 x 23cm cake

An all time favourite recipe, all the girls retain the memory of cooking their first Victoria Sponge. It is one of the tasks we set to any prospective cook when doing a day's trial. This traditional Victoria Sponge only has jam in the middle and a sprinkling of caster sugar over the top but we deviate sometimes from the classic Victoria Sponge by adding a vanilla butter cream or fresh cream to the middle if asked.

Ingredients

300g unsalted butter
300g caster sugar
4 eggs
300g plain white flour
2 teaspoons baking powder
6 tablespoons whole milk
4 tablespoons best strawberry or raspberry jam

Method

Preheat the oven to 180°C.
Line and grease 2 x 23cm cake tins.
Cream together the butter and sugar until light and fluffy. Gradually beat in the eggs until well combined.
Sift the dry ingredients before gently folding them into the wet ingredients.
Add the milk and mix until you have a smooth batter.
Divide the batter equally between the 2 cake tins.
Bake for 25 minutes, or until the cake is springy to the touch and a skewer comes out clean.
Allow to cool on a wire rack.
Fill the centre with strawberry jam before dusting the top with caster sugar.

# FINNS CARROT CAKE
makes 1 x 20cm cake or 1 x 21cm by 30cm tray (16 slices)

With thick, cream cheese frosting and moist sponge, this cake is as indulgent as it is delicious. This recipe makes wonderful cupcakes too.

Ingredients for the cake

280g plain white flour
280g caster sugar
3 eggs
250ml of vegetable oil
1 ½ teaspoons baking powder
1 ½ teaspoons bicarbonate of soda
1 teaspoon cinnamon
½ teaspoon salt
½ teaspoon vanilla essence
4 medium carrots, grated
125g walnut halves

Ingredients for the frosting

250g full fat cream cheese
4 tablespoons icing sugar
zest of 1 lemon

Method

Preheat the oven to 180°c.
Line and grease a 20cm cake tin or a 21cm x 30cm baking tray.
In a large bowl, sift the dry ingredients together.
In a separate bowl, beat the eggs, vanilla and vegetable oil together.
Make a well in the dry ingredients and add the wet mixture.
Stir well before folding in the carrots and walnuts.
Bake in the oven for 30 minutes or until springy to the touch.
Allow to cool on a wire rack.
To make the icing, blend the cream cheese, icing sugar and lemon zest together until smooth before spreading liberally over the cooled cake.

# LEMON & POLENTA CAKE
makes 1 x 23cm cake

A delicious tangy and syrupy cake, this is a lovely summer pudding served simply with blueberries and softly whipped sweetened cream or mascarpone.

Ingredients for the cake

150g caster sugar
2 eggs plus 2 egg whites
250ml full fat natural yoghurt
125ml vegetable oil
zest and juice of 1 lemon
150g polenta
25g plain white flour
1 ½ teaspoons baking powder
2 teaspoons poppy seeds

Ingredients for the syrup

125g caster sugar
180ml fresh lemon juice
3 sprigs rosemary or lavender

Method

Preheat the oven to 180°C.
Line and grease a 23cm cake tin.
In a large bowl, whisk together the sugar, eggs and egg whites until thick and pale.
Stir in the yoghurt, vegetable oil, zest and juice of the lemon.
Slowly fold in the polenta and poppy seeds along with the sifted flour and baking powder.
Mix well before pouring into the cake tin and baking for 50 minutes.

Whilst the cake is cooking, make the syrup by placing the sugar, lemon juice and rosemary/lavender in a saucepan.
Heat gently until the sugar dissolves.
Strain into a jug, reserving the rosemary/lavender to decorate the cake.
Remove the cake from the oven but leave it in the cake tin, using a skewer to make a number of holes in the cake. Pour the syrup over the cake.
Allow the cake to rest in its baking tin for an hour so that the syrup is fully absorbed before removing and allowing it to cool on a wire rack.
Place the sprigs of rosemary/lavender on top of the cake to decorate.

# WHITE CHOCOLATE & PISTACHIO COOKIES

This recipe makes 1 log. You can wrap this log in cling film and store it in the freezer to be used when required: simply cut as many ½cm cookies as you need and cook from frozen, replacing the remaining dough back into the freezer.

Ingredients

250g plain white flour
200g caster sugar
200g soft unsalted butter
200g white chocolate drops
100g pistachios
2 medium eggs, lightly whisked
½ teaspoon bicarbonate of soda

Method

Preheat the oven to 160°C.
Line a 21cm x 30cm baking tray with greaseproof paper.
In a bowl, cream the butter and caster sugar together until pale and fluffy.

Slowly incorporate the eggs to the creamed butter and sugar.
Sift the flour and bicarbonate of soda before folding them gently into the
mixture using a plastic spatula or wooden spoon.
Add the pistachios and chocolate chips and mix.
Roll the mixture into a log 4cm in diameter and chill in the fridge for at least
30 minutes.
Cut the dough into ½cm slices.
Bake for 5 minutes until lightly golden brown.
Remove from the oven and cool on wire racks.

# MARISA'S SHORTBREAD
makes 25 biscuits

This is an extremely useful recipe. The biscuits can be cut into any size or
shape to decorate plates at tea-time or accompany mousses such as the lemon
and ginger mousse on p. 192. Alternatively, they can be sandwiched together
with whipped cream and summer berries for an elegant pudding. This recipe
has a high sugar content so only cook the biscuits until they are lightly
golden brown – any longer and the shortbread will burn. At Finns, we cut
our shortbread into small seasonal shapes.

Ingredients

175g plain white flour
110g soft unsalted butter
50g caster sugar

Method

Preheat the oven to 180°C.
Line a 21cm x 30cm baking tray with parchment.
In a large bowl, cream the butter and sugar together.

Sift the flour into the butter and sugar and rub together until the mixture resembles breadcrumbs. Tip the mixture onto a work surface and knead to form a smooth ball of dough. Use a little flour to prevent the dough sticking but not too much as this will compromise the recipe.

Wrap the dough in cling film and place in the fridge for about 20 minutes.

Roll the dough out to a 2mm thickness.

Cut into the desired shapes and bake until lightly golden.

Cool on wire racks before tossing in plenty of caster sugar.


# BUTTERMILK CARAWAY RUSKS
makes 24 rusks

This South African recipe makes 24 chunky fingers. Shaped like a cantucci biscuit, I often double the recipe and store the surplus in a biscuit tin to bring out when friends drop by for unexpected elevenses or tea.

Ingredients

1kg plain white flour
2 eggs, lightly whisked
200g caster sugar
190g unsalted butter, melted
500ml buttermilk or natural yoghurt
1 teaspoon caraway seeds
1 teaspoon baking powder
1 teaspoon salt

Method

Preheat the oven to 180°c.
Line a baking tray with greaseproof paper.
Sift the flour, salt and baking powder into a large bowl. Add the caraway seeds.

In a separate bowl, mix the eggs, sugar and buttermilk/yoghurt together.
Fold the wet ingredients into the dry ingredients using a plastic spatula or
metal spoon.
Knead the mixture lightly, adding the melted butter very slowly.
Shape the dough into a large rectangle, 2cm thick.
Bake for 30 minutes.
Allow to cool on a wire rack.
Turn the oven down to 80°c.
Cut the rusk into 24 short fat fingers and return to the oven to dry out for 6
hours or over night.

## "Hi Darling" Muesli
makes 1kg

A number of years ago, Colette's mother sent her an e-mail. It read "Hi
Darling, Muesli," followed by a recipe. That was all. A hybrid of her recipe,
Finns muesli is for darling daughters everywhere.

Ingredients

350g oats
50g dessicated coconut
80ml vegetable oil
100ml runny honey
80g sesame seeds
80g chopped apricots
80g dried cranberries
80g pecan nuts
80g sunflower seeds
80g pumpkin seeds
80g linseeds

Method

Pre-heat the oven to 180°C.
In a large bowl, mix the oats, coconut, oil and honey.
Place the mixture in a large baking tray and bake for about 25 minutes or until golden and crunchy, stirring the mixture twice during baking.
Add the seeds, nuts, chopped apricots and dried cranberries to the mixture.
Allow to cool completely before storing in airtight containers for up to 2 months.

# The Amber Foundation

Since 2007, Finns has supported The Amber Foundation, a charity which sets out to transform the lives of homeless, disadvantaged and unemployed young people. The Foundation works with those who have a history of drug or alcohol abuse, many have been involved in criminal activity or have recently emerged from prison. The people who run it are excellent, committed and responsible and their focus is on giving these young men and women a chance to sort out their problems and to rebuild their lives. They usually leave one of three residential homes after six months now in control of their futures: motivated, supported and ready for work. The majority succeed and look back on their time at Amber as the turning point in their previously haphazard lives.

What I like about Amber is their ethos of keeping busy and working together, learning to build friendships, trusting and respecting each other as well as trusting and respecting authority. A huge importance is placed on the activities which the Amberteers undertake, many of which we took for granted in our own childhoods.

The following list, printed on the back of the Amber writing paper, details activities and interests which the volunteers encourage and help the Amberteers to enjoy and experience:

*Read the papers Health Diary Weather Draw how something works Play cards Friends Table tennis Local newspaper Modelmaking Budgeting Reading Clean clothes A4 Folder Trees Get up early Exercise Places of interest Diet Imaginary portfolio of shares Cricket Learn a language Swimming Go on a boat Think positively Painting Write a poem Driving lessons Write your CV Bake bread Make a plan Go on a train Talk to people Certificate Walking Musical instrument Galleries Follow* a sport Help others 5 minute talk Go on a bus Communication skills Send off for some information Science Drawing Bonfire Write a letter to your local paper Singing Manners Sport Running Tennis Cooking Flora Design something Have a day off Filmshows Photography Have a party Knots Grow plants Repair a machine Appearance Paper aeroplanes Maps Barbecue Current affairs First Aid Birth certificate Research the job you would like to do Museums Croquet Design your house Visit a factory Passport Football Post office savings account Listen to the radio Get letters arriving Set your goals Morals Watch the sunrise Interview practice Acting Fauna Citizenship Astronomy Letters Talk to local employers Music Countryside Count your blessings Have fun Civilisation Law Bowls Pinhole camera Night in the open Camping Dog Theatre Health

All the money from our canvas bag sales goes to Amber and I make no bones in asking anyone who wants to steer their money in a good direction to contact me or them, http://www.amberweb.org/.

# Recipe List

Starters

Spinach roulade with smoked salmon and cream cheese p. 111
Celeriac remoulade with crispy prosciutto and apple p. 113
Lemon and dill celeriac with tiger prawns p. 114
Marinated and seared tuna with courgette ribbons and pink peppercorns p. 115
Pea falafel with rocket and pea shoots p. 116
Figs with robiola and parma ham p. 118
Beef carpaccio p. 118


Fish

Salmon with basil pesto p. 120
Salmon with broad beans, chilli and dill p. 122
Salmon with ginger and almonds p. 123
Salmon fish cakes with cucumber and tomato salsa p. 124
Luxury fish pie p. 126
Cod with chorizo, cherry tomatoes and olives p. 128
Cod with prawns and dill p. 129
Creamy mustard cod p. 130
Prawn and ginger egg fried rice p. 131


Poultry

Coronation chicken p. 133
Pesto yoghurt chicken p. 135
Chicken fillets in lemon and tarragon p. 136
Pea and herb chicken p. 137
Chicken with prunes and leeks p. 138
Breaded chicken escalopes with aïoli p. 139
Sweet Moroccan chicken casserole with dates, almonds and raisins p. 140
Thai green curry p. 142
Coq au vin p. 144

Puddings

Baking